VLADIMIR PUTIN

AND RUSSIAN STATECRAFT

VLADIMIR PUTIN

AND RUSSIAN STATECRAFT

ALLEN C. LYNCH

SHAPERS OF INTERNATIONAL
HISTORY SERIES

Edited by Melvyn P. Leffler, University of Virginia

Potomac Books
Washington, D.C.

Library of Congress Cataloging-in-Publication Data
Lynch, Allen, 1955–
   Vladimir Putin and Russian statecraft / Allen C. Lynch. – 1st ed.
      p. cm. – (Shapers of international history series)
   Includes bibliographical references and index.
   ISBN 978-1-59797-298-7 (hardcover)
   ISBN 978-1-59797-587-2 (electronic edition)
   1. Putin, Vladimir Vladimirovich, 1952-2. Putin, Vladimir Vladimirovich, 1952–
Political and social views. 3. Putin, Vladimir Vladimirovich, 1952–Influence. 4.
Presidents–Russia (Federation)–Biography. 5. Statesmen–Russia (Federation)–
Biography. 6. Russia (Federation)–Politics and government–1991-7. Soviet
Union–Politics and government–1953–1985. 8. Soviet Union–Politics and
government–1985–1991. I. Title.
   DK510.766.P87L96 2011
   947.086'2092–dc22

                                                         2011013945

Potomac Books
22841 Quicksilver Drive
Dulles, Virginia 20166

First Edition

10 9 8 7 6 5 4 3 2

For Mom and Dad

CONTENTS

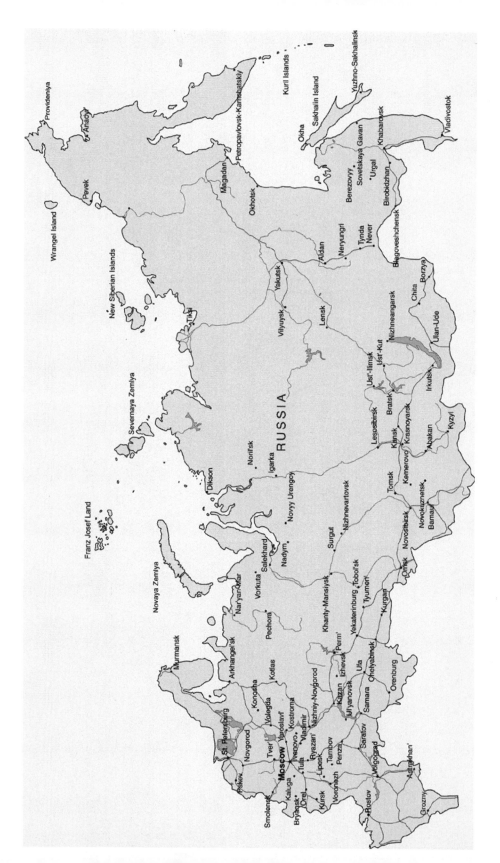

SERIES EDITOR'S FOREWORD

As human beings, we are interested in our leaders. What they say and do has a profound impact on our lives. They can lead us into war or help to shape the peace; they can help promote trade and prosperity or sink us into poverty; they can focus on fighting terror or combating disease, or do both, or neither.

We also know that they are not as strong and powerful as they pretend to be. They, too, are enveloped by circumstances that they cannot control. They are the products of their time, buffeted by technological innovations, economic cycles, social change, cultural traditions, and demographic trends that are beyond their reach. But how they react to matters they cannot control matters a great deal. Their decisions accrue and make a difference.

This series focuses on leaders who have shaped international relations during the modern era. It will consider those who were elected to high office and those who were not, and those who led revolutionary movements and those who sought to preserve the status quo. It will include leaders of powerful states and those of weak nations who nevertheless had the capacity to influence international events extending well beyond the power of the country they led. This series will deal with presidents and dictators, foreign secretaries and defense ministers, diplomats and soldiers.

The books in the series are designed to be short, evocative, and provocative. They seek to place leaders in the context of their times. How were they influenced by their families, their friends, their class, their status, their religion, and their traditions? What values did they inculcate and seek to disseminate?

How did their education and careers influence their perception of national interests and their understanding of threats? What did they hope to achieve as leaders and how did they seek to accomplish their goals? In what ways and to what extent were they able to overcome constraints and shape the evolution of international history? What made them effective leaders? And to what extent were they truly agents of change?

The authors are experts in their field writing for the general reader. They have been asked to look at the forest, not the trees, to extrapolate important insights from complex circumstances and to make bold generalizations. The aim here is to make readers think about big issues and important developments, to make readers wrestle with the perplexing and enduring question of human agency in history.

In this book, Allen Lynch does a wonderful job summarizing Vladimir Putin's rise to power and analyzing the practice of his statecraft (as we have seen it to date). We get a vivid portrayal of the impact of World War II on Putin's family and the scars it bequeathed. We see the young Vladimir as a poor student and a school yard bully—impulsive, bossy, even prone to violence. We see him seeking purpose and finding it in music, language study (German), and, most of all, exercise and judo. Putin learned self-discipline, developed focus and ambition, and made career choices that surprised all those who knew him.

Lynch deftly traces the impact of Putin's career with the Committee for State Security (KGB), his posting in the German Democratic Republic (East Germany) during its turbulent disintegration in 1989 and 1990, and the lessons he derived as he watched the Union of Soviet Socialist Republics (USSR) dissolve. Putin returned to Leningrad, furthered his education, developed critical ideas about the requisites for a successful economy, and decided to leave the KGB. In the middle chapters of this volume, Lynch cogently describes Putin's career trajectory in St. Petersburg city politics. He highlights Putin's move to Moscow, analyzes his role in the politics of the Russian state, and examines the actions that impelled President Boris Yeltsin to choose Putin as his successor.

According to Lynch, Putin mattered. He was chosen to lead a state that was in the midst of an economic freefall, a government that was corrupt and ineffective, and a people who were demoralized. Russia was beleaguered by civil strife and secessionist movements, especially in Chechnya. Its military was in a state of decay, its international standing in disrepute. Buoyed by a spectacular rise in oil prices, Putin consolidated power, intimidated his foes, crushed the secessionists, and established financial solvency. He sought good relations with Germany and France, reached out to the United States after the 9/11 attack, and hoped to integrate a resurrected Russian economy into a thriving international marketplace. Rebuffed, as he saw it, by the George W. Bush administration, he embarked on a more independent course, flexing Russian power and seeking to assert Russian authority in the "near abroad"–that is, the USSR's former domain.

Lynch skillfully analyzes the attributes and liabilities of Putin's leadership. We see the man seeking to reconcile his penchant for a strong state with his belief in a market economy, his respect for the West with his pride in Russia, his concern with order with his understanding of democratic legitimacy. We see him as a leader trying to resurrect the power of his country and revitalize its influence in international relations. Putin's legacy is still uncertain, because his role is still incomplete. But Lynch provides a marvelous framework for assessing the career of a man who is self-consciously seeking to reshape Russia's place in international history.

Melvyn P. Leffler

PREFACE

Vladimir Putin marked his twelfth year as Russia's ruler in 2011. The duration of his reign equals that of Franklin Roosevelt as U.S. president (1933–1945). During these twelve years, the impressions that most Americans and Russians developed about Putin and his policies diverged almost completely. Americans, as well as Europeans, tend to see Putin as an aggressive authoritarian, nostalgic for the old Soviet order and ruthlessly bent on eliminating opposition at home and asserting Russian power abroad. Most Russians, by contrast, view Putin as having staunched the bleeding of the Russian state, presided over the recovery of the economy after a decade of depression, and defended Russian dignity in the councils of nations. Moreover, in the face of the world's worst economic crisis since the 1930s, Russians see that Putin kept their country afloat, in striking contrast to the economic collapses under Mikhail Gorbachev and Boris Yeltsin. And Americans would be surprised to learn that Putin sees himself as committed to the modernization and even Europeanization of Russia.

In part, each side is reading the same facts and interpreting them through its own experiences and preoccupations. Thus, while Westerners condemn Putin for centralizing political power at the expense of Russia's formal political institutions and civil society, they generally underestimate the extent to which Russia had ceased to function as a coherent state by the time Putin assumed power in 1999, after nearly a decade of botched liberal reforms. This disorder helps explain why, in almost every instance where Putin has been faced with the short-term choice of control or liberty, he has chosen the apparent certainties of command over the risks of freedom. The dangers of disintegration were real, and Putin's preference for order reflected the mood of Russian society. Conversely, Russians, while grateful for the increase in their living standards under Putin, tend to gloss over the fact that in the past decade Russia has become ever more dependent on oil and natural gas exports, and raw materials more generally, for its prosperity and stability. Such dependency jeopardizes the country's long-term prospects for modernization, in part by fueling massive corruption. Putin, while aware of the unsustainability of this path over the long run, was either unable or unwilling to change course during twelve years in power.

In foreign policy, Americans fear that Putin has launched Russia on a cool if not another cold war with the United States. They cite the Russian-Georgian war of August 2008 as a case in point. Russians, however, see Russia beleaguered on all sides by America's relentless geopolitical advance along its immediate borderlands, and believe that Putin checked U.S. influence there for the first time in the post-Soviet period. Even U.S. president Barack Obama's famous "reset" of American-Russian relations has not relieved Russian foreign policy elites of a fear that the United States continues to compete for influence along Russia's historical borderlands.

This interpretive biography of Vladimir Putin seeks to explain why Americans and Russians have such contrasting views of the Russian ruler's achievements and to offer an independent evaluation of Putin's record in the Kremlin. It argues that Putin's choices as Russia's leader have been informed by a complex interplay of Russia's post-Soviet circumstances and Putin's own socialization and experiences before arriving in the Kremlin. Given the highly personalistic nature of Kremlin politics, the preferences of the top leader matter much more than they do in well-institutionalized political systems. Among Putin's character traits are devotion to the state, pride in country, a fierce sense of personal honor and loyalty, and a ferocious work ethic, as well as a profound fear of disorder. They were cultivated in his family, school, and profession. Over time, he acquired an understanding of central defects in the Soviet system, especially the economic isolation from the world that rendered most of the Soviet economy backward, wasteful, and uncompetitive. (He was much less bothered by Soviet political repression.)

Most decisively, Putin spent six years (1990–1996) as deputy mayor of his hometown St. Petersburg, Russia's second-largest city (population: 5 million).

In this capacity, Putin understood that the Soviet era was definitively over and that a new synthesis between state and market had to be developed for a post-communist Russia. To a remarkable extent, Putin as president applied models of political economy, as well as international relations, that he had developed in St. Petersburg's city hall and as part of a study group at the St. Petersburg State Mining Institute. As deputy to Mayor Anatoly Sobchak, one of Russia's foremost champions of democracy and rule of law, Putin also concluded that Russia needed a diplomacy that furthered the country's economic ambitions to the maximum extent possible.

The organization of this book follows from its basic assumption that Putin's statecraft flows from the interaction of personality and circumstance. The first half of the book takes a standard, mainly chronological approach to Putin's life and career, while the second half takes a more analytical and topical approach to a series of issues in Russian domestic and foreign policy between 1999 and 2009.

Chapter 1 examines Putin's formative years, beginning with his family background and tracing his early socialization in his family, in school, at university, and in the KGB, the Soviet secret police. Chapter 2 analyzes his understudied but critical post-Soviet years as a deputy mayor of St. Petersburg, concluding with his move to Moscow in mid-1996. Chapter 3 looks at his Moscow years as a lieutenant of successive Kremlin officials, culminating in Boris Yeltsin's appointment of Putin as prime minister in August 1999. Chapter 4 treats Putin's initial months as prime minister and then acting president in some depth, insofar as they intersect with the explosive problem of the Chechen war of secession, which proved decisive in Putin's rise to the Russian presidency.

I shift perspective somewhat in chapters 5 and 6, which deal analytically with domestic policy and foreign policy. In domestic affairs, the focus is on the methods by which Putin built an authoritarian political machine in the course of stabilizing the state and rectifying the country's economic and financial prospects. In foreign policy, I examine Putin's efforts to assert the prerogatives of power from a weak hand. In particular, I focus on his attempted partnerships with the United States and then with Germany and France, as well as the continuing challenges that he has faced in asserting Russian predominance across the post-Soviet periphery. In the conclusion, I attempt to assess Putin's record of accomplishment and his economic, political, and diplomatic legacies for Russia's future. This appraisal is admittedly a tentative exercise, as Putin, at the time this book was written, continues to wield decisive power in the Kremlin and may well continue to do so for the indefinite future.

Along the way, the reader will become familiar with a series of tensions and paradoxes that structure much of Putin's life and his tenure in high office. These forces include: (a) the impulsiveness of his early nature versus the impressive sense of discipline and self-control that he first learned in mastering Oriental martial arts; (b) his deep and genuine respect for personal honor and loyalty versus a corresponding ruthlessness toward those seen as violating those values; (c) an abstract understanding of the requisites of modernity, including economic, civic, and political liberty, versus an emotional attachment to discipline, order, command, and control; (d) an impressive cosmopolitanism, including flawless German, versus an often crude provincialism when pressed on issues of emotional import, like Chechnya; (e) a refined capacity to deploy the forms of political accountability, including elections, while minimizing the chances of meaningful political opposition; and (f) in foreign policy, a sophisticated understanding of Russia's dependence on global trading and financial markets and its diplomatic implications of restraint versus a crude form of power politics in dealing with Russia's weaker neighbors along the country's borderlands.

An appreciation for such paradoxes in Putin's personality and policies can help flesh out the often cardboard-like image of Putin in the West and place his record as Russian leader in the context of his time and circumstances. It is my hope that the reader will come away with a better understanding of why so many Russians were genuinely alarmed that Putin might actually observe the terms of the Russian Constitution and step down as president in spring 2008, and why he actually did so.

ACKNOWLEDGMENTS

I would like to express my thanks to the following friends and colleagues for their invaluable help in making this book possible: first of all, to Melvyn P. Leffler for having proposed the book and rendered the most conscientious service in critiquing the manuscript in various forms; to Feng Shao-lei, dean of the School of Advanced International and Area Studies and director of the Center for Russian Studies at East China Normal University, Shanghai, for having arranged a sabbatical stay in the spring of 2008; to Ronald Donaldson, Erik Hoffmann, Daniel Kelly, Andre Liebich, Reneo Lukic, Hugh Ragsdale, Paul Shoup, Paul B. Stephan III, Yuri Urbanovich, Denise Walsh, Gustav Weber, Ann Womack, and Brantly Womack for their close reading and commentary on the manuscript in various forms; to an anonymous Russian reader for extraordinary courtesy and invaluable criticism; to Herman Schwartz for having passed along priceless data on arcane matters of Russian political economy over the years; and to Tatiana Omeltchenko-Tatarchevskiy for having obtained much needed books in Russia when I could not. It should go without saying, but bears repeating, that I am inexpressibly grateful to my wife, Tullia, for her own reading and commentary on the manuscript as well as for her constant encouragement and support. *Per Tulliam ad astra!*

INTRODUCTION

"Those [Russians] who do not regret the downfall of the Soviet Union have no heart; those who want to bring it back have no brains."

—Vladimir Putin, May 5, 2005[1]

As Russia's leader, Vladimir Putin has enjoyed popular approval ratings, ranging from 65 to 87 percent since 2001, that would be the envy of any U.S. president. That he should have been able to enjoy such sustained popular legitimacy flies in the face of broadly held views in North America and Europe about the stifling of liberal politics and Western political values that has undoubtedly marked Putin's tenure as Russia's ruler. Throughout that period, beginning in August 1999 when Boris Yeltsin appointed him prime minister, Russia witnessed a series of remarkable transformations at home and abroad. A complex pattern emerged in which the Russian economy recovered from a prolonged and devastating depression, the country assumed a more activist stance in world affairs, and Putin—faced with a state that had virtually ceased to govern—built a powerful political machine that was as popular at home as it was controversial abroad. At the same time, a more centralized government was not necessarily an efficient one. By mid-2011 it seemed at best uncertain whether, in the long run, Putin had done anything more than reinforce Russia's fateful dependence on oil, natural gas, and other natural resources for its wealth and stability. Had Russia simply become a "petrostate," similar to Venezuela or Nigeria but with Eurasian characteristics?

1

In the political sphere, Putin centralized power around his own person, whatever his formal title of the day. In the process, he eliminated what remained of genuine sovereignty in Russia's eighty-three federal districts. While Russian and Western liberals decried this repression, most Russians supported it, seeing regional governors more as corrupt and semi-criminalized feudal barons than as responsible leaders. At the same time, Putin drove private business and financial interests, or oligarchs, out of the presidential administration and insisted that in running the government, the state's interests take priority over those of large-scale, private enterprises. He transformed the Duma, or parliament, into an extension of his own preferences and has ensured that the judiciary remains the plaything of the government in matters of political concern to it. Finally, Putin successfully harnessed the Russian media–above all, television news with a national reach–so that most of the population, most of the time, heard only the official interpretation of politically sensitive news.

In this light, the notion of a division of powers and checks and balances–which are formally guaranteed in the Russian Constitution–elicits ridicule among Russians in the know. Russian society remains largely apathetic, if not supportive of the trends just described, and shows little evidence of unease at Putin's concentration of power. From time to time, inconvenient journalists and defectors die mysterious deaths at home and abroad, with little enthusiasm from either prosecutors or the government to bring the killers to justice. At times Putin has even blamed the victims for the embarrassment that their deaths have caused the government, as in the case of the murder of the brave journalist Anna Politkovskaya. And one foreign politician, Ukraine's president Viktor Yushchenko, has been poisoned in circumstances pointing plausibly to elements in the Russian government.

Centralizing power, however, has not always led to more effective government. Between 1999 and 2004, Russia was wracked by a series of terrorist acts exceeded in scale and casualties only by the September 11, 2001, attacks in the United States. In the case of the September 2004 Chechen-related terrorist seizure of an entire public school in Beslan in southern Russia, the police and federal authorities were unable to assert effective control over the hostages' hundreds of distraught civilian relatives surrounding the school. This lapse proved to be a major factor contributing to the disaster that ensued and resulted in more than three hundred hostages killed. By 2009 a series of large-scale Chechnya-based terror attacks outside the North Caucasus indicated that the region was far from pacified: in March 2009 two bombings in the Moscow subway killed 40 and wounded 100; in November 2009 a train was destroyed near Bologoye, killing 28 and wounding 97; and in January 2011 an attack at a Moscow airport killed 35 and wounded 180.[2]

Similar indicators of the fragility of the Russian state abound. Corruption and mismanagement of public institutions have reached levels dwarfing those of the unfortunate 1990s. Despite more than a decade of impressive economic growth between 1999 and mid-2008, the Russian economy and government remain more dependent on receipts from energy and other raw material exports than ever, and the precariousness of its economic accomplishment was underscored in the fall of 2008 when the fledgling Russian stock market lost 70 percent of its value after the price of oil fell from $145 to $35 per barrel. Despite having grown 8.1 percent in 2007, the last full year before the 2008 economic crisis, the Russian economy declined by 7.9 percent in 2009. This 16-point negative swing in growth was the largest in the world, thereby underscoring a fateful dependence on world oil prices, reinforced by widespread economic mismanagement. (In contrast, Chile's economy, comparably dependent on the export of raw materials, especially copper, declined by just 1.6 percent in 2009, while that of Saudi Arabia, the quintessential petrostate, actually grew by 4.2 percent in 2009.[3] Direct investment in the country's crumbling industrial, transportation, and human resources infrastructures has languished, with the network of paved roads actually contracting by 9 percent in the Putin years.

In foreign policy, after a bold and largely unrequited overture to the United States after the September 11, 2001, attacks, Putin began to cultivate anti-Americanism by way of both justifying his lost gamble and appealing to a powerful sense of frustrated nationalism in a society still recovering from the humiliations of the Soviet Union's collapse. Putin opposed, albeit behind the skirts of the French and Germans, the Americans' path to war in Iraq and continued to play a double game with Iran. He claimed to be an honest broker for the United States while at the same time maintaining a major Russian program for building nuclear power plants in Iran and promising the Iranian armed forces defensive weapons that could be used to frustrate a possible U.S. or Israeli attack on Iran's nuclear infrastructure. Having acquiesced graciously to the accession of three formerly Soviet Baltic states into the North Atlantic Treaty Organization (NATO), in January 2006 and again in January 2009

Putin ordered the cessation of natural gas deliveries to Ukraine, governed by the pro-American Viktor Yushchenko, in the dead of winter. Putin eventually backed down but not before arousing the alarm of the European Union, which intervened insofar as Ukraine was also a major transit zone for the delivery of Russian natural gas to Western Europe.

Shortly after the first gas cutoff, and in a deft move, Putin co-opted Germany's former chancellor Gerhard Schroeder by inviting him to join the board of a Russian company that is building an underwater gas pipeline directly from Russia to Germany. This will allow Russia to bypass Eastern Europe and pursue an energy diplomacy of *divide et impera* toward Western Europe and Eastern Europe. By the summer of 2008, with Putin still clearly the power behind the throne, the Russian Army invaded Georgia after a convenient provocation by Georgian president Mikheil Saakashvili. Along the way Putin leveraged the secession of the Georgian provinces of South Ossetia and Abkhazia from Georgia and sent a clear signal that Georgian (and Ukrainian?) membership in NATO would not be tolerated. Also that summer and fall, the Russian government sent a naval squadron to Venezuela as a sign of solidarity with the anti-U.S. government of Hugo Chavez, reinforcing previous measures of symbolically harassing the United States by flying nuclear-capable bombers to monitor U.S. naval exercises around the globe. Finally, within twenty-four hours of Barack Obama's election as president of the United States, Russian president Dmitri Medvedev, in a statement evidently cleared by Putin, explicitly warned Obama that Russia would deploy nuclear missiles on the Polish border in the Russian exclave of Kaliningrad if Obama would not reconsider the deployment of U.S. antiballistic missile systems in Poland and the Czech Republic. (When Obama cancelled this program in September 2009, Putin dropped the threat.)

This admittedly gloomy picture of repression at home and assertiveness abroad needs to be tempered by the realization that Putin's government, while perhaps not very "good" by Western political standards, is arguably one of the best that Russia has ever had. Under Putin's administration, Russia recovered from the decade-long depression that had set in during the last years of Mikhail Gorbachev's rule. Propelled initially in late 1998 by favorable exchange rate effects following a massive devaluation of the ruble and then reinforced by a persistent upward trend in world oil prices between 1999 and mid-2008, the Russian economy grew on average 7 percent annually during the eight years of Putin's presidency. Russian gross domestic product (GDP) recovered roughly to where it had been immediately before the Soviet collapse, a process that had taken place more than a decade earlier in most of ex-communist Eastern Europe. Per capita income also doubled, and the percentage of Russians enjoying reasonably comfortable lives gradually increased, reaching perhaps a quarter of the population by 2008, an unprecedented figure in Russian history. In the course of a decade, the Russian car market became the largest in Europe.[4]

While growing energy revenues were central to this success story, Putin also took a series of specific steps that contributed significantly to reestablishing a degree of stability in public affairs that had seemed irretrievably lost just a few years earlier. By 2001, when the price of oil was rising but still modest compared to what was to come, Putin introduced a major tax reform with a 13 percent flat tax, which was calculated at a rate that Russians would actually pay. As a result, the Russian government's finances began to assume some form of stability as revenues more closely matched expenditures. By 2008 the Russian federal government's budget had been well in the black for several years running. Putin also passed a major land reform bill through the Duma that allowed for the sale of land for the first time in Russian history. Putin's government established several reserve funds under state control for both emergencies and long-term investment projects, accumulating more than $200 billion by mid-2008. By then, the Russian government had also amassed nearly $600 billion in foreign exchange reserves (mainly dollars and euros), the third highest in the world. Unlike Yeltsin's government in the late 1990s and Gorbachev's before him, Putin was thus in a position to cushion the shock to the Russian economy after world oil prices collapsed during the global crisis of 2008–2009, spending 12 percent of the country's GDP in various forms of economic stimulus.[5]

Relatedly, earlier Putin had paid off the entirety of Russia's external sovereign debt, much of which had been assumed in the Gorbachev period. Moscow and the centers of other major cities, such as St. Petersburg and Nizhny Novgorod, had become visibly affluent, highlighting a degree of prosperity unique in the country's history. Consequently, Putin enjoyed a genuine degree of charismatic popularity and legitimacy, so much so that a majority of Russian society as well as the political class in 2007 worried that Putin actually might step down as president in conformity with the Russian Constitution.

In foreign policy, Putin revealed a deeper pragmatism and prudence than Western fears of a new cold war implied. Having backed the United States in the war against the Taliban in Afghanistan, after which the Americans pocketed most of his concessions, Putin did not hesitate to oppose American policy but seldom did so directly or alone. On the Iraq War, for instance, Putin took care to see that Russia belonged to an antiwar coalition that included the key U.S. NATO allies of Germany and France. Despite Russia's historically fraught relations with Poland, Putin took two bold steps to reframe ties. While in Warsaw on September 1, 2009, on the seventieth anniversary of the Nazi invasion of Poland, Putin denounced the Nazi-Soviet Non-Aggression Pact of 1939, under which Stalin had covered Hitler's eastern flanks while the latter invaded Poland, with Stalin joining him seventeen days later. Then, on April 7, 2010, Putin attended a joint ceremony with Polish prime minister Donald Tusk at the memorial for 20,000 Polish army officers murdered at Stalin's orders in the Katyn forest and publicly admitted–to substantial outcry at home–Soviet responsibility for the deed.[6] As a result, notwithstanding all their remaining difficulties, Polish-Russian relations are on a fundamentally better track.

In these respects, Putin's Russia differs dramatically from that of the Soviet Union, which found itself enmeshed in a costly and dangerous isolation in world affairs during Putin's formative years as a counterintelligence officer in the State Committee on Security (KGB). More generally, by presiding over the balancing of the federal budget, the liquidation of the country's sovereign debt, and the progressive consolidation of the state's control over the bulk of Russia's vast oil and natural gas complex, Putin established a foundation for Russian influence abroad and self-respect at home that had been lacking during the previous decade of Russia's attempted rapprochement with the West. Fluent in German and well versed personally on German affairs, Putin reinforced Russia's energy relations with the Federal Republic of Germany, the most important power in the European Union and Russia's single most important and stable bilateral relationship. Where he clearly overreached, as when he cut off gas supplies to Ukraine, Putin quickly acquiesced to the European Union's diplomatic intervention.

The widespread umbrage in the United States at Russia's military intervention in Georgia in August 2008 tends to gloss over the fact that Russia had been reduced to fighting for its sphere of external influence along its post-Soviet border with Georgia. There, a pro-American president aimed to join NATO as rapidly as possible and no doubt believed that he had the Americans' backing as he attempted to remove Russian peacekeeping troops from South Ossetia by force of arms. Russia under Putin had been reacting not simply to a series of bilateral disputes with the government of Georgia but more broadly to the apparently ceaseless process of NATO expansion toward Russia's borders, encompassing in the worst-case scenario Ukraine as well. Russia's carefully prepared counter-intervention undermined those prospects, and for the first time in the post-Soviet era, a Russian leader had succeeded in posting limits to the eastward expansion of NATO's security sphere.[7]

The broad lesson that Russian elites had drawn from the 1990s, when NATO waged war against Russian clients in Bosnia and Serbia, was that it is not communities of values and interests but rather vectors of raw power that frame Russian-Western and especially Russian-American relations. Translating that conclusion into a decisive Russian victory over Georgia—viewed in Moscow as an anti-Russian, U.S. client state—Putin boosted his already impressive popularity among his countrymen. Most Russians were impressed by the way that Putin had made Russia a subject and not merely an object of world politics. Even before that conflict, a major Russian feature film released in 2007 titled, simply, *1612*, clearly implied that Putin could be compared to Czar Mikhail Romanov and the latter's historical role in unifying the nation against mortal Western threats.

Not for the first time, a Russian leader possessed a reputation abroad that was almost diametrically opposed to his image at home. Nobel Peace Prize laureate Mikhail Gorbachev continues to be lionized in the United States and Western Europe for his key role in ending the Cold War. Within Russia, however, Gorbachev is reviled by democrats for not having broken decisively with the Communist Party and by nationalists for having brought about the disintegration of the Soviet Union and the unification of Germany in NATO. Revealingly, in the Russian presidential elections of 1996, Gorbachev received 0.5 percent of the vote. Reversing the frame, Putin is today largely reviled in the United States and Western Europe for having centralized authoritarian and nationalist power in his own person while Russians widely admire him for having done exactly that. Every society tends to perceive others through the prism of its own values, prejudices, and internal preoccupations.

One aim of this book is to help us understand how a man like Vladimir Putin, a quintessential product of the Soviet system, can evoke such passionate and contradictory emotions in Russia and in the West, respectively. Another is to demonstrate just how much of Putin's worldview is prefigured in his biography and in particular the progress of his socialization. Themes that would mark Putin's tenure in office–above all, the tension between his intellectually grounded concern to prevent Russia's stagnation and his emotionally based fear of disorder and disintegration–are clearly discernible in his personal experience well before his fateful Moscow years from 1996 onward. Putin's preferences for the certainties of command over the risks of liberty are rooted in a life history characterized by the fear of losing personal and political control, as well as in his professional socialization in the Soviet secret police. His steadfast defense of the prerogatives of the state, rooted in a patriotism that is qualified by an impressive but almost soulless cosmopolitanism, traces it roots to the troubled history of his family and his country in the several decades before his birth in 1952.

1

THE FORMATIVE YEARS
(1952-1990)

"I have two natures and one of them is German."

— Vladimir Putin[1]

Vladimir Putin's biography is a quintessential Soviet success story. He trod the path of a Russian Horatio Alger hero, a wayward child of a working-class family scarred by war and death. By dint of sheer determination and hard work, he became the first member of his family to attend university, attained the pinnacle of Oriental martial arts accomplishment, and realized his boyhood dream of working for the most powerful institution in the country, the KGB.

Disillusioned by what he saw as the creeping degeneration of the communist system, Putin abandoned his career in the KGB to work for one of Russia's leading liberal democrats, St. Petersburg mayor Anatoly Sobchak, who was also his former law professor. Serving as a deputy mayor of Russia's second-largest city during a tumultuous period of economic privatization and foreign investment, Putin quickly mastered the byways of postcommunist political and economic administration.

Displaying a prodigious work ethic, can-do spirit, and intense loyalty, Putin was later called to Moscow, where he quickly came to the attention of Russian president Boris Yeltsin. Yeltsin was desperately searching for a reliable successor, one who would not only win an election but would also keep promises to shield Yeltsin and his family from prosecution for corruption or political offenses once he retired from politics. In a stunning turn of events, Yeltsin appointed Putin prime minister in August 1999 as a complete political unknown. Within months, Putin began building a powerful political machine that would catapult him and the party of his creation into national power, where they remain to the present day.

FAMILY BACKGROUND

Vladimir Putin was born on October 7, 1952, in Leningrad.[2] He became the first Russian leader since Czar Alexander III (reign: 1881–1894) not to have experienced a world war firsthand. Those who raised Putin, however, had directly and personally experienced both war and revolution. Putin's paternal grandfather, Spiridon Putin (1879–1965), hailed from peasant stock in the Tver region of central Russia, in the Volga basin some hundred miles northwest of Moscow. The Putin family still maintains a simple home there. At age twelve Spiridon and a cousin worked at an inn in Tver, and at fifteen he left for St. Petersburg to study cooking. Spiridon worked for a time as a chef at the famous Hotel Astoria in St. Petersburg, where he once served the infamous Grigory Rasputin. Rasputin, impressed with the cuisine and noting the similarity of their names, tipped Putin with a gold ruble for his fare.[3]

Drafted into the imperial army, Putin's grandfather welcomed the Russian Revolution in part because of the government's inability to stop the Germans ("they were everywhere"). After the Russian Revolution of 1917, he fled a starving capital to ride out the remainder of the war and revolution in his ancestral home in Tver. Spiridon later returned to Petrograd and then moved to Moscow. There, given his reputation as a first-class chef, he wound up as a cook in Vladimir Lenin's country dacha. After Lenin's death in 1924, Spiridon cooked for his widow, Nadezhda Krupskaya, and sister in the Lenin family compound until their deaths years later. He also cooked from time to time for Joseph Stalin.[4] In light of the potential explosiveness of Krupskaya's voice in Soviet politics (she was aware of Lenin's written "political testament" in which he severely criticized Stalin), it is almost certain that Spiridon Putin served in the employ of the People's Commissariat for Internal Affairs (NKVD), the secret police predecessor of the KGB. After Krupskaya's death in 1939, he worked as chef in a Moscow Communist Party boarding house. He survived until 1965, dying when Putin was thirteen. Of his four sons (that is, Vladimir Putin's father and three uncles), two died in the Second World War and Putin's father was crippled in action. Just one son emerged physically unscathed from the cauldron of what Russians call the Great War for the Fatherland. In addition, an aunt of Putin's was forced to work as a slave laborer for the Germans in the Baltic region.

Putin's father, also named Vladimir (1911–1999), married Putin's mother, Maria (1911–1998), when both were seventeen years old. He was drafted into the armed forces in the mid-1930s and served in the submarine corps, being discharged in 1937. Joining the Communist Party before the Nazi invasion on June 22, 1941, Putin's father volunteered for the Soviet military and defended his native Leningrad during the two-and-a-half-year Nazi siege of the city. More than a million Russians died during that time, mainly of starvation and related causes.

Putin's father engaged in especially deadly operations, serving as a commando behind Nazi lines in neighboring Estonia; the NKVD ran the twenty-eight-man search-and-destroy unit. When their food ran out, they were apparently befriended by ethnic Estonians who brought them food while also tipping off local German forces to their presence. Quickly surrounded, the small Soviet force desperately tried to escape. The Germans gunned down most of the commandos as they fled. Putin's father was one of four who survived. At one point he eluded the German search dogs by hiding underwater in a swamp and breathing through a reed.[5] Returning to the front lines, he was later wounded by a German grenade. Bleeding nearly to death, he was saved by a former neighbor, who happened to see him and carried him miles to the hospital.[6] Putin's father suffered from the effects of the wound for the rest of his life, walking with a limp. After the war, he worked as a toolmaker and a foreman in an industrial plant, making railway and subway cars. He lived until August 2, 1999, just before Putin's appointment as prime minister of Russia. Having seen his son rise so high, the father once joked, "My son is like a Tsar!"[7]

Putin's mother, Maria, worked in a factory while his father served in the navy in the mid-1930s. She bore two sons before him: Oleg, who died in infancy before the war, and Viktor, who died at the age of two from diphtheria triggered by malnutrition and exhaustion during the German blockade of Leningrad, which lasted nine hundred days. Viktor's death was so hard on Putin's mother that she never said where the child was buried. Maria, completely distraught at her second son's death, was herself left for dead of starvation and had to cry out to be rescued from a pile of corpses awaiting burial. Later, she was wounded by an exploding German artillery shell.[8] Her own mother was killed in Leningrad during an exchange of German and Soviet gunfire in the courtyard of their apartment building in October 1941.[9]

No one in Putin's family seems to have been caught up in Stalin's prolonged terror, which was carried out by the NKVD and disproportionately affected peasants and members of the intelligentsia regardless of their Communist Party affiliation. The Putins were urbanized by the 1920s, and they lived a typical Soviet working-class life. Their experience under Stalin was one that combined service to the state, including its highest leaders; a small degree of upward mobility, by comparison with life in the countryside; and an intense but shared suffering in a patriotic war. Given that Putin's father fought heroically in a combat unit run by the NKVD, forerunner to the KGB, it is not surprising that Putin himself would one day be attracted to a career in the Soviet secret services.

PUTIN'S EARLY YEARS

In 1952, at the age of forty-one, Maria gave birth to Vladimir, who was the apple of her eye. Putin himself admits that his mother doted on him.[10] She worked midnight shifts at the most menial labor, including working as a janitor, making nighttime deliveries for a bakery, washing test tubes, and shoveling snow off sidewalks and streets, in order to spend the most time possible with young Vladimir (Volodya for short).[11] Likewise, she kept him home from kindergarten and sent him to school only at the last possible minute, to first grade, when Putin was nearly eight.

Young Putin thus grew up as an only child and "spoiled," within the parameters of the hardscrabble existence of Soviet working-class life in postwar Leningrad. He lived in a *kommunalka*, or communal apartment, that was typical of Soviet urban housing at the time. The Putins occupied one room in the apartment, a fifth-floor walk-up on Baskov Lane in downtown Leningrad, and lived there with Putin's uncle and family, for a total of six people—four adults and two children—in a room of 20 square meters (215 square feet). The room was heated by a wood stove and had neither hot water nor a bathtub. The entire apartment shared the toilet, which was located outside the apartment on the landing and was freezing in the long Russian winter. The stairwell itself was full of perilous gaps and infested with rats. There was, as one of Putin's teachers Vera Gurevich said, "no room to move around."[12] Still, as the same teacher observed, "by the standards of those [postwar] days it was decent."[13]

Putin as a lad with his mother, Maria (circa 1960). Used by permission of the website of the President of the Russian Federation, www.kremlin.ru.

Secretly, in a practice common in Soviet Russia, his mother had taken him as an infant to be baptized. Secrecy was of utmost importance because Putin's father, whom Putin seldom saw given his long working hours,[14] was by then a local party functionary. If Putin's baptism came to light, the father might have lost his job in the officially atheist Union of Soviet Socialist Republics (USSR). Much later, in 1993, Putin's mother would give her son his baptismal cross to have it blessed at the tomb of Jesus Christ during his official visit to Israel. Putin obliged and has not taken the cross off (at least in public) to the present day.

Putin grew up among neighbors who were practicing Jews and befriended them. Their prayers in Hebrew could often be heard on the Sabbath. A Jew, Mina Moiseyevna Yuditskaya, played a decisive role in Putin's life as his German teacher.[15] Years later, during an official visit to Israel to meet with émigré Jewish veterans of World War II, President Putin contacted Yuditskaya, who had left the USSR for Israel in 1973. Putin asked her to tea and later, at a state banquet, introduced her "as my teacher" to former Israeli president Moshe Katsav. Shortly thereafter, Putin presented the aged and infirm Yuditskaya with a new, fully furnished, easily accessible, and free apartment in downtown Tel Aviv. (Putin did not publicize this act, which only came to light three years later in the Russian press.[16]) As president, he has consistently distanced himself from the ugly displays of anti-Semitism that still dot the Russian public landscape.

Putin grew up in a public atmosphere of proud and intense Soviet patriotism. The war had been a true collective trauma and an understandable source of pride for those who lived through it. His parents had suffered terribly, but their lives were no more difficult than those of millions of other Soviet citizens between 1941 and 1945. Putin was very proud of his family's links to Lenin and of his parents' heroism during the war. He loved his Soviet homeland, all the more so as the Communist Party's propaganda systematically exploited the victory over the Nazis as the cornerstone of the regime's legitimacy. Soviet patriotism was a much more compelling theme than the alleged economic benefits of communism in a society beset by perpetual shortages of routine consumer goods.[17]

Putin's father was a true believer in core communist ideals and fostered his son's pride in Soviet achievements.[18] When Putin was five, the Soviet Union launched Sputnik, the world's first artificial space satellite. Thereafter, the Soviet Union repeatedly bested the United States with firsts in space exploration, culminating in the spring of 1961 with the successful launch and recovery of Yuri Gagarin from earth's orbit. The Soviet government understandably exploited the handsome Gagarin to emphasize its achievements. Russians' genuine pride in Soviet space accomplishments has lasted to the present day.

Given these astounding accomplishments, how could an impressionable boy like Putin fail to be affected by the aura of patriotism penetrating every corner of Soviet society? Shortly thereafter, he came to love spy stories appearing in books, television, and the movies. Financed by the KGB, the Soviet secret services were presented in these media as playing a heroic role in the victory over Nazi Germany. One such film, the 1968 release *The Shield and the Sword* directed by Vladimir Bosov, completely mesmerized the teenage Putin. He was intrigued by the drama's Soviet double agent infiltrating Nazi Germany and thwarting the Nazis' war plans.[19] He read every spy novel he could and resolved to pursue a career in the secret services.

But he still had much growing up to do. As a boy, he was impulsive, bossy, even a bully. He was a schoolyard punk, prone to violence. Undisciplined, he was a poor student, and the Soviet Pioneer organization initially rejected him as uncontrollable.[20] This exclusion is truly remarkable inasmuch as the Pioneers, comparable in social and political function to the Hitler Youth, aimed to include all Soviet youth and sought to socialize them to the purposes of the Soviet system. Schooled in the "jungle" of the street, young Putin could not adjust to rules. Possessing explosive physical energy, he spent time between classes bounding up and down stairwells. Once, Putin was hauled before a neighborhood "comrades' court" and judged for acts of petty delinquency. His father, by then a respected local party official, begged for leniency and pledged responsibility for Putin's future conduct. The court released Putin into his father's stern custody.

Putin regularly received 3s (Cs) in physics, chemistry, algebra, and geometry. But in sixth grade, when he was thirteen years old, he began to change. He was attracted to subjects and activities for which willpower alone did not suffice. He began to play the guitar, singing songs by the remarkable Russian bard Vladimir Vysotsky, whose lyrics were antiestablishment but not antiwar. He started studying German seriously. Most important of all, he was won over by Oriental martial arts. He mustered the spiritual and physical discipline needed to progress in judo and later in karate and sambo, a Russian form of martial arts.[21] Perhaps Putin recognized the gap between his impulsive nature and his modest physical frame, which was typical among children of mothers who suffered from malnutrition during the Nazi blockade of Leningrad. Putin came to see that judo was much more than a set of techniques for victory in physical combat; rather, it was an entire "philosophy . . . a serious and useful art." He learned that he needed to be smart, cunning, and disciplined, as well as strong, in order to master a situation. Sports dragged him off the streets and changed his life.[22]

Putin's school grades quickly improved. He showed a particular aptitude for the social sciences and humanities, including German. But he had not relinquished his dream of becoming a Soviet secret agent. Indeed, in the ninth grade, Putin approached the local branch of the KGB, asking for an appointment to discuss his career prospects. The receptionist put him in touch with a dutiful senior agent, who advised him to join the military or study law but in any event not to contact the agency again. Putin decided then and there to study law, which in Soviet Russia was a low-paying and low-prestige field. Against the advice of his coaches and the wishes of his parents, who preferred that he pursue an engineering track, in 1970 Putin enrolled in the International Division of the Department of Law at Leningrad State University. As a child of the working class, he was admitted, in effect, as an affirmative action student.[23]

Putin led a full, successful life in college and was committed to his legal studies. His undergraduate thesis, "The Most Favored Nation Trading Principle in International Law," prefigured an attentiveness to the economy and international relations that would mark his presidency. He took a course on economic law taught by the liberal scholar Anatoly Sobchak, who later became Putin's mentor in the St. Petersburg city hall.[24] All the while, Putin cultivated his expertise in martial arts, attaining the rank of master of sambo in 1973 and master of judo in 1975. He later earned a black belt in karate. In 1976 he became the Leningrad city champion in judo and once fought world champion Vladimir Kullenin, losing a close match on points. His coach believed that had Putin stayed focused on judo instead of his career in intelligence, he would have become the Soviet and even European champion.[25]

Putin's entire public persona in college was that of a hardworking, disciplined, athletically impressive but socially unobtrusive and apolitical man. He did join the Communist Party of the Soviet Union while in college, a standard enrollment for anyone with professional aspirations in the USSR of that time. He did not gamble or, so far as we can tell, drink heavily (a point that tends to be confirmed by Putin's later relatively abstemious habits). He did like European pop music, including the Swedish group ABBA.[26] He also left a girl "at the altar," a subject that he has never elaborated on in public and for which he has expressed neither regrets nor remorse. (In this connection, his friend Sergei Roldugin has stated that young Putin "could not express his emotions."[27]) He neither took a leading role in any of the customary communist youth organizations nor appeared to have been an informer to the KGB. In short, Putin had assumed a low-key personality profile almost ideally suited to the requirements of the KGB.

JOINING THE KGB

The KGB, which had evidently been keeping tabs on Putin, formally contacted him in the fourth of his five years in college. He was thrilled to be on a probationary track and was more determined than ever to do what it took to make the grade. That grade was quite steep: Putin was the only student in his law class whom the KGB selected. When the KGB finally offered him a job, Putin accepted enthusiastically. By his own admission, he was unaffected by the murderous legacy of the Soviet secret police and its complicity in Stalin's terror. Putin was also quite cautious. His friend Leonid Polokhov later said that Putin surprised him only twice in his life—when he joined the KGB and when he left it. Other friends, whose families had suffered greatly under Stalin, were shocked that Putin would join the agency, and he took pains to assure them that he would never tolerate "illegal" acts of repression against innocent citizens.

So, inspired by a romantic image of the KGB, the twenty-two-year-old Putin began his career in the agency in 1975 and worked initially in the sec-

Putin throws a Japanese judo expert during a judo exercise at the Kodokan Judo Hall in Tokyo (September 4, 2000). Putin has a black belt in the sport. Noboru Hashimoto/Corbis/Sygma

retariat of the Leningrad city and regional KGB, perhaps the agency's most notoriously hard-line division in the country.[28] Putin harassed dissidents and sought to contain the few outbreaks of political dissent that occurred in the city. In one case that Putin cites with professional pride, he and his colleagues pre-empted a small demonstration by showing up disguised as putative dissidents themselves and fooling the Western media, which promptly dispersed once the KGB saboteurs left. When the handful of real dissidents arrived later, they had no audience. Such "staged farces" would later become a hallmark of Putin's own political machine.

After six months of such work, Putin was transferred to operations. There-after, he worked in Leningrad until 1984 in counterespionage and eventually in foreign counterespionage, which gave him the chance to deal with foreigners, including the many sailors frequenting Leningrad's port. He kept tabs on them and perhaps even recruited some for the Soviet cause. Much of his work also involved routine debriefings of Soviet citizens who traveled abroad on business.

Given the proximity of Leningrad to noncommunist Finland, Putin might have had significant responsibility. But he did not. For nearly eight years, he languished in Leningrad. Oleg Kalugin, a KGB defector and Putin's boss in Leningrad, confirms that most agency activity in the region consisted of petty monitoring of foreign travelers and investigating rumors. "In twenty years of operations," Kalugin states, the Leningrad KGB's foreign counterintelligence division "captured not one spy."[29]

PRIVATE LIFE

In 1980, Putin met his future wife, Lyudmila, an airline stewardess on the Kaliningrad–Leningrad route. The poorly dressed Putin, who only revealed that he worked for the "police," impressed the young woman by the ease with which he was able to procure tickets to any show in town, including that of the famous comic Arkady Raikin. In time, he further impressed Lyudmila with his "manly character." She later said that she liked his open heart, modesty, "Christian morals," and deep, inner sense of responsibility toward his friends and supporters. Most of all, Lyudmila thought that Putin was "reliable," that he would always make the right decision in a crisis. Dreaming of a harmonious family life, she reflected,

> I had my ideas of how a couple in love should live together: they would share common interests, they would confide in each other about what was going on at work, advise each other, share the management of the household, jointly raise and educate the children, with whom they would spend their free time. That's how I imagined family life. It was an idealized notion of mutual understanding and harmony in family relationships.[30]

It never occurred to Lyudmila that her husband would be unable to talk to her about anything related to his career. She only learned that Putin was a KGB officer, rather than an ordinary policeman, from the wife of one of Putin's colleagues. Nonetheless, she married Putin fully aware of his professional situation and that in effect she was marrying the KGB as well.[31] But his marriage proposal, after a courtship of three years, was so stilted and complicated that she thought at first they were breaking up. According to Lyudmila, the proposal scene went as follows:

> *Putin* (seated with Lyudmila): "Well, my dear, you know my personality. It is not an easy one to get along with. And now, as a matter of principle, you will, it seems, have to define your situation in life."
>
> *Lyudmila* (trembling, believing that he has just broken with her): "You know, I have decided. I need you."
>
> *Putin*: "Well, then, I propose that we get married. I love you. Do you agree?"
>
> *Lyudmila*: "Yes, I agree."
>
> *Putin*: "If it's all right then we'll set the date for the wedding for July 28th, three months hence."[32]

On July 28, 1983, Vladimir Putin and Lyudmila Shkrebneva were married in the customary civil ceremony. The wedding party lasted two days—the first day was for family and friends, the second for Putin's KGB colleagues, who for reasons of confidentiality could not attend a more public affair.[33] After a long honeymoon in the Crimea, the newlyweds shared a two-room apartment, measuring about three hundred square feet, with Putin's parents in Leningrad. Soon, they had two daughters, Maria and Katya, born in 1985 and 1986, respectively.

By all accounts, they were loving and devoted parents. In 1986, Lyudmila defended a thesis, "Participles in the Spanish Language," at Leningrad State University. Her facility in languages was passed on to Maria, who speaks Chinese and Japanese. She and her sister, Katya (concentrating in biology), attended Moscow's famous Deutsche Schule at the German Consulate in 1996–1999. After Putin became prime minister, they were educated privately, for reasons of security.

KGB ASSIGNMENT—DRESDEN

Within a year of his marriage, the KGB sent Putin to Moscow, where he trained at the agency's center for foreign counterintelligence in preparation for an assignment abroad. Shortly after Maria's birth in 1985, Putin was assigned to Dresden, East Germany. A major, he worked in the Fourth Department of

Putin and his wife, Lyudmila, with their firstborn child, Maria (Spring 1985). Used by permission of the website of the President of the Russian Federation, www.kremlin.ru.

Putin and his wife during a happy moment at the Taj Mahal (October 2, 2000).
Kapoor Baldev/Sygma/Corbis

Foreign Counterintelligence, which covered German-speaking Austria, Switzerland, the Federal Republic of Germany (West Germany), and the German Democratic Republic (East Germany). Sources differ as to why Putin was assigned to the provincial city of Dresden in East Germany instead of to Berlin or West Germany itself. Most likely, Putin's own explanation suffices: he accepted the assignment because it was the quickest route abroad.[34] As a child of the Soviet working class instead of the ruling *nomenklatura* (elite), Putin did not have the contacts that might have landed him a more prized placement with in East Berlin, not to mention in West Germany, Austria, or Switzerland.

Life in communist East Germany made a big impression on the Putins. It was their first time abroad, and the young couple was struck by the comparatively prosperous lifestyle there. They lived in a spacious and comfortable apartment together with families of the East German Ministry for State Security (Stasi, or secret police) employees. They enjoyed what Lyudmila Putin termed "an abundance of [consumer] goods" without having to wait in long lines, which were typical outside of shops in the Soviet Union. Putin was allotted a weekly quota of four quarts of the German beer (Radeberger Pils) and quickly gained ten pounds. He received part of his pay in hard currency—that is, in U.S. dollars, West German marks, or Swiss francs—and was frugal enough that, upon his return to Leningrad in 1990, he was able to buy a Volga, an upscale Soviet sedan.

Although surrounded by East German secret police colleagues and their families, Putin claims to have seen no evidence of the infamous Stasi persecution of East German citizens. Lyudmila, who hailed from Kaliningrad, formerly Prussian Koenigsberg, felt at home in Dresden. Both Kaliningrad's and Dresden's architecture combined traditional German motifs with endless rows of functionalist apartment buildings rapidly built after the massive destruction each city suffered during the final months of the Second World War.[35] Lyudmila still remembers her years in Dresden fondly.

As a KGB major in Dresden, Putin made occasional trips to Berlin and even, at least once (according to West German security cameras), to West Germany itself. With his command of German, Putin's main task in Dresden was to monitor itinerant Western businessmen and scientists, with the hope of recruiting them for Soviet industrial and military espionage and of gleaning general political intelligence. Soviet intelligence focused on the Eurofighter combat aircraft for the North Atlantic Treaty Organization (NATO). Dresden was also the home of a fledgling East German computer industry, so there was no short-age of potential contacts. But many of Putin's activities in East Germany re-main inevitably vague. He probably spent time monitoring the activities of Soviet troops based in the country, as that was a routine KGB function in East European communist countries. It is known, for instance, that Putin at times contacted local Soviet military commanders.

Throughout his time in East Germany, Putin operated in the open, without a pseudonym, working closely with his colleagues in the East German Stasi. He enjoyed his work in East Germany and was promoted three times in five years for his service, earning several commendations from the East German Stasi. His colleagues recall him as devoted, loyal, and efficient. He did not come across as a careerist. Indeed, had he been one, Putin would have pulled all possible strings to be promoted out of Dresden. His Soviet colleagues even nicknamed him "Stasi," in deference to his Teutonic work ethic.

At times, in the absence of the chief, he served as acting head of station. But Putin does not contradict the often-made judgment that he "was a low-ranking officer in a job of little importance." Markus Wolf, the East German spymaster, has stated that the Dresden division of the KGB was the least signifi-cant branch of the agency in East Germany. Wolf neither met Putin nor even heard of him in connection with the KGB's activities in the country. Indeed, all evidence suggests that Putin was unknown to the leadership of the KGB itself. As one astute Russian observer notes, "Putin did not make a brilliant career for himself in intelligence. Had he, he would likely today be living off of his pen-sion and puttering in the garden, like so many of those who did have a brilliant career there."[36]

THE END OF AN ERA, 1989

In December 1989, a month after the Berlin Wall fell, an event occurred in Dresden that perhaps more than any other marked Putin's future sensibilities toward power and authority. An enraged East German mob, having already stormed the main Stasi office on the Elbe River, marched through the cool, dark, late autumn air to the villa housing the KGB office for Dresden. The an-gry crowd, armed with weapons seized from the Stasi armory, was threatening to storm the KGB building. As it turned out, Putin was acting head of mission at that moment, as his boss had gone into town.

Putin was now on the horns of an explosive dilemma. On the one hand, if the crowd seized the KGB's building, with its countless secret files, including damning evidence of East German collaborators with the Stasi and KGB, Putin (if he survived) would undoubtedly stand trial before a KGB tribunal for dereliction of duty and be shot. On the other hand, if the crowd was determined to rush the building, it could only be stopped with massive bloodshed, which he wanted to avoid if at all possible.

As a first, precautionary step, Putin ordered the skeleton crew of KGB personnel to stand at the windows while ostentatiously armed with Kalashnikov submachine guns. Putin then called the local Soviet military command, explained the situation, and requested the immediate dispatch of troops. He calculated that an overwhelming display of force would suffice to prevent an outbreak of violence from the crowd. What transpired next shook Putin to the core.

General: "I can't send you the troops, I have no orders from Moscow. I'll call back and explain everything."
When the general did not call back, Putin phoned again.
General: "I asked Moscow but Moscow is silent."
Putin: "But what are we going to do?"
General: "In any event, I can't give you any help."

At that moment, Putin understood, in his own words, "as clearly as possible, that we were abandoned and that no one was making any decisions."[37] As Putin recalled more than a decade later, from the vantage point of the Russian presidency, "It seemed to me as if our country no longer existed. It became clear that the Soviet Union was in a diseased condition, that of a fatal and incurable paralysis: the paralysis of power."[38] He was on his own.

Putin then headed to the gate, where he spoke to the crowd in German and identified himself as an interpreter. Had Putin followed his standing instructions to the letter, he would have ordered the building barricaded, set up an armed perimeter defense (with troops he did not have), and refused all negotiations with the crowd. Whatever bloodshed might have flowed, Putin would have been technically covered for having followed existing regulations. Instead, while preparing a demonstrative display of force at the windows by the few troops at his disposal and ordering the immediate burning of sensitive personnel documents, Putin–against the advice of his KGB colleagues–began to engage the crowd. Putin was clearly violating his instructions.

In Putin's account, the exchange went as follows.

Crowd: "Who are you and what is this building?"

Putin: "It's a Soviet military facility." (Putin wanted to avoid the topic of the KGB, which, just as its Stasi counterpart, was a much more explosive topic than that of the Soviet military in East Germany.)

Crowd: "Why are there cars with German license plates on grounds?"

Putin: "By agreement with the government."

Crowd: "And who are you?"

Putin: "I'm the interpreter." (Again, Putin wanted to avoid a confrontation over the KGB and its East German Stasi partner. The same crowd had just ransacked the Dresden Stasi office.)

Crowd: "Interpreters don't speak German so well!"

Putin: "I plead with you to behave decently and not to trespass. We have specific rules of conduct, and once again I repeat that this has nothing to do with the Stasi or the East German armed forces. This is a Soviet military facility, which has extra-territorial status."

German eyewitness accounts add a detail that Putin omits. They say Putin himself brandished a pistol and declared dramatically, "I am a soldier and ready to die!"[39]

At that point Putin, with his small, armed escort, turned around and returned slowly to the building. The crowd hung around for an uncomfortably long time but began to disperse after evidently giving up the idea of storming the building. By this point, the local Soviet military commander had decided to send troops to reinforce the security of the KGB headquarters, after which the crowd disappeared into the night.

This encounter with the East German crowd and the paralysis of Soviet power seared itself into Putin's consciousness and undoubtedly framed many of his subsequent decisions. At its most prosaic, the affair underscored for Putin in ways that he had not yet truly grasped the decomposition of the Soviet state that was already under way as an unintended byproduct of Gorbachev's reforms. "I understood then," Putin has said, "that if such events were to take place in the Soviet Union, I wouldn't be able to find work anywhere." More broadly, the haunting refrain that Putin received that night, "Moscow is silent," continues to resonate for Putin and those in his immediate political entourage. "It touched me deeply," Putin admits.[40]

As Russia's president, Putin committed himself to curing, as he saw it, the "paralysis of power" that infected the late Soviet Union as well as post-Soviet Russia in the 1990s. In virtually every instance where Putin has had to choose between the liberties of individuals, social groups, and society as a whole on the one hand and the power of the state on the other, Putin has bet on the state. As the German Russian observer Boris Reitschuster has characterized it, "As President, Putin has never forgotten the dramatic events in Dresden."[41] These events would decisively affect his future policies.

The collapse of Soviet power that Putin witnessed in East Germany seems to have had the kind of traumatic effect on his subsequent political-psychological development that Alexander III experienced when terrorists assassinated his father, Czar Alexander II, in 1881. As Reitschuster has put it, "Both felt themselves to be victims of the weakness and incapacity of the state, on which they had set such great store. In each case, Alexander and Putin, respectively, firmly decided that the power of the state had to be strengthened."[42]

2
IN ST. PETERSBURG'S CITY HALL
(1990–1996)

"It's better to be hanged for loyalty than for betrayal."
— *Vladimir Putin, 1996*[1]

That Vladimir Putin worked in the KGB is generally known in and outside Russia. Yet the corresponding assumption that people often make—that as Russia's ruler Putin has simply been acting as a KGB man—is belied by the profound effect of the ten years that he spent in St. Petersburg and Moscow after resigning from the agency in 1990. (The KGB finally accepted his resignation the next year.) During that crucial decade, Putin became fully involved in Russia's profound and convulsive transformation from a centrally planned economy to a market economy as well as from a one-party state to a competitive, multi-party political system. During this time Russia also emerged from a position of extreme isolation in the global economic system and became an integral part of the international political economy. As a deputy mayor of St. Petersburg, Putin not only plunged headlong into Russia's unprecedented post-Soviet transformation but also acquired invaluable administrative and political experience and substantive knowledge in whole new fields, such as energy economics. He also became part of a network of strategically placed associates who propelled his career all the way to the Russian presidency. Once there, Putin drew heavily on that St. Petersburg network to staff his administration and to help him govern Russia.

Putin's six years spent managing his hometown also helped him crystallize his post-Soviet worldview. While never converting to the political liberalism

27

of his boss and mentor, Anatoly Sobchak, Putin accepted the irreversibility of the Soviet Union's collapse and came to terms with the market and with private property as the proper foundations of the Russian economy. He now saw Russia's isolation from the world economy as the chief defect of the Soviet system, as it rendered the bulk of the economy noncompetitive and extremely wasteful. At the same time, Putin was aghast at the destabilizing consequences when the state, at the national level, had largely ceased to govern. He joined an intellectual circle at the St. Petersburg Mining Institute that advanced the idea that state management of Russia's vast raw materials economy and, above all, the fuels sector was central to Russia's economic recovery and future development. Putin developed real expertise in this area and drew upon it heavily while serving as Russia's president.

Finally, these St. Petersburg years were a public stage on which Putin revealed character traits that would inform his tenure as president and prime minister. These qualities included a highly developed sense of personal honor, loyalty to a fault toward those who helped him or had been faithful in his service, a devotion to duty that verged on "workaholicism," and an impressive disregard for his own career when its progress came into conflict with what Putin regarded as the higher values of duty, honor, and country. Less admirably, he also showed himself to be impatient and abrupt with those who did not live up to his expectations, pitiless toward those whom he regarded as having betrayed his trust or broken an understanding, and seemingly incapable of displaying empathy or other emotions of genuine warmth, even toward intimates.

RETURN TO RUSSIA

Putin returned to Russia with his family in the winter of 1990, six months short of completing his five-year tour in East Germany. After the Berlin Wall came down, the Soviet KGB closed most of its installations in what remained of the German Democratic Republic. The Soviet agents who had worked with the Stasi, Putin included, were "outed" when the personnel archives of the East German secret police were published. Having arrived in Dresden with the rank of major, Putin left as a lieutenant colonel.

Upon his return to the Soviet Union, he was offered a position in Moscow at the headquarters of the KGB's foreign intelligence operations. Someone motivated by sheer careerism would have jumped at the opportunity to work in the center. Yet Putin was a Leningrader by birth, upbringing, education, and early professional socialization. Both of his aged parents still lived there. If he had moved to Moscow, moreover, his family's living conditions there would have been uncertain. Given the extreme scarcity of housing in the capital, it could be years before he found a satisfactory apartment there. Putin, therefore, returned to Leningrad, in spite of Lyudmila's clear enthusiasm for going to Moscow.[2]

Putin remained in the KGB until after the failed coup against Gorbachev in August 1991. He turned down an assignment in the Leningrad KGB's personnel division and obtained an appointment as a special assistant for international affairs to the dean of Leningrad State University. He worked there undercover, monitoring the comings and goings of foreign students and their interactions with Soviet students. The KGB normally assigned such jobs to agents who were near retirement; that it was assigned to the thirty-eight-year-old Putin meant that he had now become, in effect, a has-been.[3]

Putin understood his situation. He began to think about writing a dissertation, searched for an academic adviser, and started to review the relevant literature. He mused that he might go into teaching or business.[4] After several months working undercover at his alma mater, he was introduced by a former professor at the university to Anatoly Sobchak, the liberal chairman of the Leningrad City Council.[5] Putin impressed Sobchak, who offered Putin a staff job at city hall. Putin jumped at the chance.

Putin worked for Sobchak for six years (1990–1996), mainly serving as a deputy mayor. His experiences decisively influenced his outlook. He quickly came to believe these principles:

- The Soviet system had exhausted its possibilities of development, and there was little chance of its resuscitation.
- Market economics and international economic relations were central to St. Petersburg's and Russia's prospects.
- A strong guiding hand by government was necessary to monitor a market economy and to avoid socioeconomic disruption and chaos.
- Russia's vast natural resources were central to the country's economic prospects.
- Russia was relatively poor and weak in the context of international relations and could not afford confrontations with the postindustrial democracies.
- Personal loyalty was central to establishing effective networks of governance.
- Open-ended electoral contests were distasteful and potentially dangerous.

SOLDIER TO SOBCHAK

Putin's political godfather, Anatoly Sobchak (1937–2000), was the son of a railway machinist and an accountant. His grandfather was arrested on political grounds in 1939; his paternal grandmother was Czech. He was a distinguished professor of economic law at Leningrad State University, where he taught but did not know Vladimir Putin well, if at all, in the early 1970s. In the Gorbachev period, Sobchak emerged as one of the strongest and most charismatic advocates of democratization, going to the lengths of broadcasting lectures on legal topics on Leningrad television. In 1989, in the first relatively open elections in Soviet Russia since 1917, Sobchak was elected to the Congress of People's Deputies on a reform platform and quickly emerged as the chairman of the Interregional Group of liberal-minded deputies in the congress. Overnight, Sobchak—a charismatic public speaker—became one of the most famous personalities in the Soviet Union. The televised proceedings of the congress mesmerized the country with its open criticism of such hitherto taboo topics as the KGB's abuses of power. In May 1990, Sobchak became chairman of the Leningrad City Council, at which point he asked Putin to join his staff and handle foreign economic affairs.

Sobchak and Putin each agree on the substance of the delicate and critical conversation that ensued: Sobchak did not trust anyone on his team. He wondered if Putin could be of help and asked him to leave the university to work on his staff. Sobchak had already spoken with the dean of the university and requested that Putin be allowed to move to city hall. The conversation continued as follows.

> *Putin:* "Anatoly Aleksandrovich, I would do this work with pleasure. It sounds interesting. I even want to do it. But there is one thing that will evidently be an obstacle to this move."
>
> *Sobchak:* "What's that?"
>
> *Putin:* "I have to tell you that I am not just an advisor to the Dean but . . . a line officer of the KGB."
>
> *Sobchak* (evidently surprised): "Well . . . the hell with it! . . . Look, I need an assistant. To be honest, I'm afraid to go out into the lobby; I have no idea of what kind of people I've got there."[6]

Before closing the deal, Putin asked his KGB supervisors for permission to leave his university post. The agency, overwhelmed with processing thousands

Russian politician and Putin's mentor Anatoly Sobchak in St. Petersburg (September 1991). Putin also took Sobchak's law course at Leningrad State University in the early 1970s.
Vittoriano Rastelli/Corbis

of intelligence officers returning from Eastern Europe, was only too happy to be rid of him and immediately granted his request.[7]

In May 1990, Vladimir Putin, still technically in the KGB's ranks, became Sobchak's adviser for international affairs. He took charge of registering all foreign businesses operating in St. Petersburg and supervising their financial dealings, a task involving staggering sums of money. In late August 1991, Sobchak, now elected mayor, appointed Putin as the chairman of the city's Commission on Foreign Affairs. A few months later, Putin became a deputy mayor as well, rising to first deputy mayor in 1994. This position made him the third-highest-ranking official in the St. Petersburg city government. Putin coordinated all relations with the "structures of power," including the military, the police, the district attorney, and customs officials. He also managed diplomatic relationships, as well as dealings with nongovernmental social organizations.

For much of this time, given Sobchak's frequent and protracted absences and his preoccupation with national affairs, Putin assumed the functions of acting mayor. He supervised the drafting and implementation of countless international business deals and policy reforms. These transactions did not always go according to plan, and no doubt many profited handsomely from Putin's admitted inexperience in these matters. During his attempt to establish municipal oversight over a series of casinos, for example, the city was cheated. In another case, the city was fleeced for $120 million for two shipments of cooking oil. Although during this period his mother bought a choice apartment at an exceptionally low price at a city auction, Putin didn't seem to enrich himself personally.[8] In the one specific public charge of corruption that was brought against him, Putin sued in court for slander and won.

In the daunting new world of early post-Soviet public administration, Putin's accomplishments in St. Petersburg were impressive. They included:

- attracting plants owned by Coca-Cola, Wrigley, and Gillette;
- signing some six thousand joint ventures with foreign firms by 1995;
- establishing a significant foreign banking presence, with banks allowed 100 percent foreign capitalization, and overseeing the opening of branches of Dresdner Bank and the Banque Nationale de Paris, the first foreign bank branches in all of Russia;
- legalizing the sale of land;
- permitting the virtually free privatization of residential apartments;
- renovating the airport, reforming the customs house, and opening an international trade center;
- organizing a large-scale program of food relief in the winter of 1992 and coordinating deliveries from the United States, Germany, Japan, France, and Great Britain; and
- strengthening the municipal banking system sufficiently so that in 1998, when the Russian financial system imploded, St. Petersburg's city banks survived, whereas their Moscow counterparts did not.[9]

Putin frequently encountered foreign statesmen, both in St. Petersburg and abroad. Accompanying Sobchak, he often acted as his interpreter with German speakers. Putin met, among others, German chancellor Helmut Kohl, British prime minister Margaret Thatcher, U.S. secretary of state James Baker, and President William (Bill) J. Clinton multiple times each, as well as Jimmy Carter, Henry Kissinger, Al Gore, Ronald Reagan, French president Jacques Chirac, Queen Elizabeth II, and nearly all of the leaders of the post-Soviet states. During his six years of working in the St. Petersburg mayor's office, Putin accumulated a vast amount of administrative and executive experience, more, in fact, than anyone in Boris Yeltsin's entourage.

Rumors understandably circulated at the time that, given Putin's career in espionage, he was in reality a KGB plant in the liberal Sobchak's office. This claim seems unlikely. The KGB was then in the process of headlong fragmentation, being almost fully absorbed by the repatriation of thousands of agents from formerly communist East-Central Europe. Given the agency's prior willingness to assign Putin to what amounted to a sinecure at the dean's office at Leningrad State University, Putin's supervisors likely placed little stock in his switch to city hall. Moreover, not only had Putin submitted his resignation to the agency, but he also then contacted a friend who was a television producer and, in order not to be blackmailed, stated on the air that he had indeed been a professional KGB agent. Whatever operational use the agency might have had for Putin was now definitively destroyed. He had been publicly exposed twice, first in East Germany and now in Russia itself.[10]

Sobchak, one of the fiercest public critics of KGB abuses in Russia, affirmed that in six years of service Putin never gave him any reason to doubt his loyalty.[11] Indeed, Sobchak had such high confidence in Putin that he routinely left him a sheaf of the mayor's blank official letterhead with Sobchak's signature at the bottom. In a famous episode, two KGB agents proposed to Putin that they forge Sobchak's signature on official city letterhead. Putin pulled out the letterhead with Sobchak's signature already on it. Said Putin to the astonished agents, "You see, the man trusts me. And I will not abuse that trust." He thereupon wrote an outraged letter to the city's KGB headquarters.[12]

Putin was not corrupt, at least in the conventional, venal sense. His modest and frankly unfashionable attire bespoke a seeming indifference to personal luxury. While as deputy mayor, he had acquired the use of the summer dacha of the former East German Consulate and even installed a sauna unit there, but when the house burned down in the summer of 1996, his $5,000 life's savings burned with it. To have accumulated only $5,000 in five years as deputy mayor of Russia's second-largest city and largest port, when hundreds of less well-placed Russians were enriching themselves on government pickings, implies something other than pecuniary motives behind Putin's activities. Commenting on her husband's way of life, Lyudmila Putin noted: "He was never at home. . . . I was left alone with the kids, my in-laws and a miserable apartment. We didn't have a stick of decent furniture. And we hardly had any money to buy anything with."[13]

In sum, Putin was honest, certainly by Russian standards. He lived simply and worked diligently. And while he displayed impressive loyalty to Sobchak, he never shared Sobchak's principled commitment to liberal values. On the whole, his performance in St. Petersburg was successful.

INSIGHTS INTO PUTIN'S CHARACTER

These years revealed other aspects of Putin's evolving character. In response to a series of incidents, minor and major, Putin displayed a propensity for decisive and effective action. Refusing to flinch in times of crisis, he also assumed high risks to support those he had pledged to defend, whatever their politics. In the course of these episodes, Putin also demonstrated an unsentimental acceptance of the passing of the Soviet order.

During the August 1991 anti-Gorbachev coup attempt, Putin played a key role in saving Leningrad for the democrats. The coup, which lasted but three days, was carried out on August 19. That same day Mayor Sobchak arrived on a flight from Moscow. The Leningrad KGB, which supported the Moscow coup, planned to arrest Sobchak immediately upon landing. Putin got word of the plan and took decisive and preemptive action: he organized a handful of loyal troops and met Sobchak at the airport, driving the car right up to the plane's exit ramp. The KGB turned back, not wishing to risk an open confrontation with Sobchak's armed entourage.[14]

After this failed coup, a group of neo-communist organizations occupying offices in the fashionable Smolny district decided to hoist the red hammer and sickle communist flag from a pole on the building's roof. The goal was to mock the town hall democrats, now including Putin, who could see the Soviet flag from their office windows. Putin repeatedly ordered that the flag be taken down, but each time a new flag appeared the next day. An angry Putin dispatched a crane to the scene and had the rooftop flagpole itself cut off at its base.[15]

In September and October 1993, when Russian president Boris Yeltsin was locked in a do-or-die confrontation with the Russian parliament, Sobchak secretly sent Putin to Moscow with a group of special forces to assist Yeltsin. While Putin did not take part in the fighting that ensued (with more than 150 killed on the parliamentary side), he did investigate and overhaul the staff around the revolt's leader, Gen. Albert Makashov.[16]

In 1996, Putin was in charge of Sobchak's campaign for governor of St. Petersburg. In a hotly contested race, Putin witnessed the systematic use of smears and slander, the streams of dirty money, and the underhanded but perfectly legal political tactics that defeated Sobchak in a tight race. Putin was shaken to his core. Accused by a foe of Sobchak's of having purchased a million-dollar villa in France, Putin sued for slander and won his case in court a year later.

During the election, President Yeltsin's office—fearing Sobchak's national reputation and his ambition—intervened in the St. Petersburg campaign, dropping incriminating leaflets against him throughout the city by helicopter. After the election, the winner, Vladimir Yakovlev (also one of Sobchak's deputies), was impressed by Putin's professionalism and asked him to remain on the senior staff. In a striking display of loyalty toward Sobchak, Putin declined, declaring, "It's better to be hanged for loyalty than for betrayal."[17]

After the election, Sobchak's opponents, including highly placed members of Yeltsin's administration, pressed corruption charges and prepared court proceedings against Sobchak. By early November 1997, Sobchak was under indictment. Putin, who had now been called to Moscow and appointed Chief of the Main Inspectorate of the Presidential Administration, undertook a secret and clearly illegal operation to whisk Sobchak out of the country to France, where he would not only avoid imprisonment but also would be able to undergo a difficult operation for a serious heart condition.[18] On the night of November 3, 1997, Putin, who did not consult Yeltsin and kept the affair completely secret, went to St. Petersburg. He personally arranged for the medical papers, including Sobchak's entire medical history; obtained travel documents; and secured a special Finnish medical aircraft, at a cost of some $30,000, to transport Sobchak out of Russia. Only a handful of trusted associates from St. Petersburg military, police, and intelligence units were implicated in Putin's conspiracy. By the afternoon of November 7, Sobchak was safely in Paris.[19]

When Putin became acting president in early 2000, an ailing Sobchak was allowed to return to Russia. Putin closed his criminal case. Sobchak died in his bed in February 2000, one month before Putin was elected president of Russia. Putin felt deeply indebted to Sobchak, and his conduct toward Sobchak, even when his former democratic boss had no power and when Putin had much to lose, bears out the extent to which Putin placed personal gratitude and loyalty above many other considerations, including his own career.

Putin's rescue of Sobchak, perhaps more than any single event, opened his advance to the Russian presidency. Boris Yeltsin, in spite of his antipathy toward Sobchak, noticed. As Yeltsin wrote in his memoirs:

> When I learned that it was Putin who had transported Sobchak out of the country, I had a complex reaction, for he was risking not just himself [but

his position in my administration]. On the other hand, his deed elicited deep human respect . . . Knowing as I did the need to remove [then prime minister Yevgeny] Primakov, I was constantly and in an agonizing way thinking, "Who will support me? Who will really stand behind me?" And finally I understood that it was Putin [who would].[20]

These episodes from Putin's early post-Soviet experience underscore the traits that defined the man as he assumed executive responsibilities for the country in the late 1990s. He understood that Russia had moved irreversibly into a post-Soviet and postcommunist period, at home and abroad. He was ready to take decisive, if at times impulsive, action when convinced of the justice of his position. He displayed an impressive ability for making executive decisions, taking care with respect to operational and logistical details. He revealed an impressive capacity for loyalty and gratitude toward those who advanced his career, and he did not hesitate to violate the law in both letter and spirit in order to protect his friends. He built up and exploited a political network based on his St. Petersburg/Leningrad contacts and developed a visible distaste for free elections. Finally, Putin's deep and continued training in Oriental martial arts undoubtedly reinforced his remarkable work ethic, one distinguished by uncanny focus and discipline, traits that would soon serve him well in the snake pit of Kremlin politics.

FROM ST. PETERSBURG TO MOSCOW

The most immediate consequence of Sobchak's electoral defeat in the summer of 1996 was that Putin was now out of a job. It was around this time that Putin, anxious to burnish his credentials, submitted a "candidate's dissertation" (roughly between an American master's thesis and a PhD dissertation) titled "The Strategic Planning of Regional Resources under the Formation of Market Relations."[21] Interestingly, Putin did not mention the dissertation in a series of extensive interviews published in 2000. Indeed, it is difficult to see how he could have found the time for advanced graduate study when he was the acting mayor of Russia's second-largest city. The thesis, moreover, reveals a familiarity with advanced mathematics that is utterly absent in Putin's academic record. He was at best a C student in math and excelled only in the social sciences and in German. Of the 140 pages (Russian version) of the thesis, at least 16 pages are lifted almost verbatim, and without specific attribution, from a

1978 management textbook written by University of Pittsburgh professors William R. King and David I. Cleland. Their volume, *Strategic Planning and Policy*, had been translated into Russian in the early 1980s.[22] Putin's thesis quickly disappeared from public view once the plagiarism was reported, and neither the Kremlin nor Putin have since commented on the matter.[23]

Very likely, and in a practice common in communist and postcommunist Europe, the thesis was ghostwritten for Putin, who used his political contacts to obtain the prestigious candidate's degree from the St. Petersburg Mining Institute. At the institute, he had been involved with a small circle of associates since the early 1990s. They all worked on various aspects of post-Soviet economics, focusing on the centrality of raw materials—in particular, on oil and natural gas—to Russia's economic development. Their work and Putin's dissertation prefigured essential components of his later political-economic strategy.[24]

Most important, in Putin's thesis, the raw materials sector and its fuels sector, comprising especially oil and natural gas, play the main role in developing the Russian economy. Putin writes:

> Mineral and raw materials represent the most important potential for the economic development of the country. . . . In the 21st century, at least in its first half, the Russian economy will preserve its orientation toward raw materials. . . . Given its effective use, this resource potential will become one of the most important pre-conditions for Russia's sustainable entry into the world economy.

Putin also stresses a number of other points. First, Russia's economic prospects require the establishment of mammoth, vertically integrated firms that are closely linked to financial institutions, which, in turn, are closely regulated by the state. Global economic processes thus require "comprehensive state support and the creation of large financial-industrial corporations which span several industries [focusing] on the resource-extracting enterprises, which could [then] compete as equals with the transnational corporations of the West." Second, the Russian state needs to do a much better job of regulating the macro economy in general and those industries, like energy, that are central to the country's prospects. Writes Putin, "The development of the extracting [raw materials] complex should be regulated by the state using purely market methods; [yet] the state has the right to regulate the process of their development and use, acting in the interests of society as a whole." Finally, he states that a purely market-based governance of the energy sector is inadvisable for Russia:

> By itself the market mechanism cannot resolve the entire range of problems reviewed, and a range of problems are to be [resolved] through scientifically substantiated state regulation. . . . Going forward, the main efforts should be concentrated on completing the creation of a unified system of [state] regulatory support.[25]

There is, of course, more texture to Putin's thesis than this truncated summary allows. For instance, nowhere does Putin propose abandoning private property as the foundation of Russia's post-Soviet economy. Nowhere does he see economic regulation by the Russian state as equivalent to the command economy of the old Soviet state. Putin is acutely aware of the debilitating competitive consequences of the old Soviet central planning system, with its enforced protectionism and absence of market-based pricing signals. He recognizes that Russia's economic prospects must be linked to the global capitalist economy. He also notes that the state's development of the energy sector cannot be its sole economic preoccupation. Indeed, the impact of the capital-intensive energy field on employment is far too low, and the dangers to Russia of becoming overly dependent on unpredictable fluctuations in global commodities prices is far too great.

But overall, Putin's dissertation reveals that while his head may have accepted the existence of free markets, his heart beat to the rhythm of command and control.[26] Putin's preference for the state's primacy over the market in the raw materials economy is striking. Whatever the precise provenance of his dissertation, very few, if any, newly minted doctors of economics would have the opportunity of translating their academic findings into political practice as quickly and as dramatically as would Vladimir Putin, once he finally made his move from St. Petersburg to Moscow.

3

TO MOSCOW AND THE TOP
(1996–1999)

"Authoritarianism is contempt for the law; democracy
is carrying out the law."

—Vladimir Putin, 2003[1]

When Vladimir Putin moved from St. Petersburg to Moscow in the summer of 1996 to begin a career in national politics, the Russian economy, society, and the state itself were in crisis. Indeed, absent such turmoil, it is impossible to imagine that Putin could ever have become Russia's supreme ruler. For all of his professional life, Putin had been a "first-rate second-rate man," an able lieutenant who advanced the interests of his superiors and who was trusted above all because he apparently lacked higher ambition. There was not an inkling in mid-1996 that in just three years Putin would be catapulted to the heights of national power. When Yeltsin did appoint Putin prime minister in August 1999, the latter was virtually unknown in the country at large. His would be a most accidental presidency.

The network of political contacts that Putin developed while working in the St. Petersburg mayoralty brought him to Moscow. Once in the capital, his personal qualities earned him ever-higher appointments. The Kremlin elites, frantically positioning themselves for Boris Yeltsin's coming succession in 2000, enlisted Putin's assistance. Those elites, and ultimately Yeltsin himself, prized Putin's industry, efficiency, mastery of detail, and loyalty. They also admired his capacity for ruthless action. Between mid-1996 and early 2000, Putin went from being an obscure subaltern in the Kremlin bureaucracy to deputy head of the Presidential Administration; chief of the FSB, or the successor to the KGB; head of the National Security Council; prime minister; acting president; and finally president.

Just as the times forged Putin's path to power, they framed the many urgent challenges that he would face once in power. These problems included the virtual breakdown of the system of governance at the national level, a decade-long economic depression compounded by a financial crash in August 1998, a persistent pattern of retreat and humiliation in foreign affairs, and an ongoing war of secession in Chechnya that threatened Russia's territorial integrity. A brief consideration of these multiple and mutually reinforcing crises will help frame the political context in which Putin came to power. Once he had it, he exercised it with striking boldness and authority.

THE 1990S: MODERN RUSSIA'S TIME OF TROUBLES

The 1990s in Russia were not only a time of prolonged economic collapse, social decomposition, political corruption, and international retreat, they were also a time when Russia's economic and political prospects became intertwined with the West, and above all with the United States, in ways that were entirely novel in Russian history. Consequently, most Russians' reactions to the domestic calamities of the 1990s, a latter-day "Time of Troubles" for Russia,[2] extended into a reaction against Western and especially U.S. models of economic and political development. Concurrently, the relentless pressure that the United States and NATO exerted to expand the North Atlantic security alliance eastward and include many of Soviet Russia's erstwhile satellite states persuaded most Russians that the West itself, driven by the United States, was positively hostile to Russia's international interests and perhaps even to its existence.[3]

In the economic sphere, between 1990 and 1998, Russia suffered a depression that was twice as severe as the Great Depression the United States and Germany suffered in the 1930s. The International Labor Office of the United Nations declared, "There should be no pretense. The Russian economy and the living standards of the Russian population have suffered the worst peacetime setbacks of any industrialized nation in history."[4] Russia's gross domestic product (GDP) in 1998 was just more than half the level seen in 1989. Money had ceased to be the preferred medium of exchange, ceding pride of place to barter transactions, and credit had virtually disappeared. Russia was ranked among the least competitive economies in the world. In the words of the World

Economic Forum, "Russia is isolated from world markets, taxation is high and unstable and there is a general disdain for the infrastructure, technology and management."[5] *The Economist* Intelligence Unit regularly listed Russia as the riskiest foreign investment destination among the countries that it tracked. Domestic and foreign capital investment had virtually dried up, and the capital stock of the country was literally wearing out. For instance, the age of industrial equipment in the mid-1990s averaged more than fourteen years old, compared to eight years in 1970.

The Russian state was being picked clean by those who ran it and had privileged access to it. To give just one shocking but typical example, in 1995–1996 the Russian government in effect auctioned off nearly 60 percent of the state's industrial assets to a small group of private financiers at fire-sale prices through a device known as the loans-for-shares scheme. Through this policy, the government borrowed some $5 billion to $6 billion from a dozen or so financial barons, or oligarchs, who in return obtained collateral rights in invaluable government economic assets. The Russian government used these funds mainly to finance Boris Yeltsin's reelection campaign and pay off pressing short-term obligations. (These commitments often related to the election campaign itself, such as meeting wage arrears for government employees, increasing pensions, and securing student scholarships just in time for the summer 1996 elections.) When the government predictably failed to pay back the loans, a handful of businessmen became fabulously rich. In other cases, assets were auctioned off to government insiders in patently rigged bids. In one example, which later became notorious but at the time was utterly routine, oligarch Mikhail Khodorkovsky obtained ownership rights in what would become Russia's largest privately owned energy company, Yukos Oil Company, for about $309 million. At the time of Khodorkovsky's arrest in 2003, Yukos was valued at $25 billion. The skyrocketing value of the company—80:1 compared to the purchase price—was representative of the fleecing of the Russian state in the 1990s.

At a time when the price of oil was dropping sharply, plummeting to nearly $10 per barrel in 1998, such practices meant that the Russian government was virtually bankrupt much of the time. It strained to pay the wages of civil servants, including judges, police, military officers and common soldiers, teachers, and professors, and often failed to perform many of the common functions of governance. This general incompetence extended to macroeconomic policy, where a disastrously implemented liberalization of prices in January 1992 led to inflation rates of 2,600 percent in 1992, compounded by 900 percent in 1993 and 300 percent in 1994. Such rates, while not quite as bad as the hyperinflation of Weimar Germany, were nevertheless sufficient to wipe out the modest life savings of a majority of Russians and reduce pensions and other state subsidies not indexed for inflation to penurious levels. Seeing political insiders enrich themselves while society at large became impoverished, the Russian population quickly labeled the U.S.-backed privatization of government-owned industries and other assets as economic "piratization."[6] In August 1998, the Russian government's finances collapsed completely, and the government defaulted on its short-term domestic and foreign obligations, wiping out most of those who had managed to recover from the earlier monetary calamity.

The consequences of such reckless mismanagement, which extended to the disappearance of a $4.5 billion credit provided by the International Monetary Fund (IMF) in July 1998, seriously damaged Russia's international standing. The IMF also cut Russia off from further extensions of direct credit. Its director, Michel Camdessus, stated publicly, "I alerted President Yeltsin that Russia will be treated exactly like Burkina Faso [one of the poorest countries in the world]."[7] By 1999, Russia's foreign debt, which included obligations assumed from the defunct USSR, totaled nearly $160 billion, or nearly 90 percent of the country's GDP as calculated in dollar terms. About half of that debt was owed to Western governments, underscoring Russia's dependency on Western forbearance. More than a quarter of the government's annual budget was consumed with servicing the interest on this debt.

Further, Russia's people were not exempt from this degradation. As was true almost everywhere in postcommunist Europe in the first years of transition, key indicators of societal health declined starkly. Birth rates plummeted while rates of suicide, death, divorce, infant mortality, and alcohol abuse among men skyrocketed. In general, people behaved as if they were discounting the future while they tried to adjust to the brave new world of postcommunist economics. Although in East-Central Europe these social indicators began to stabilize and even improve by the mid- to late-1990s, such was not the case in Russia. Life expectancy for Russian men sank to below sixty years of age and stayed there throughout the decade. By 1999, a Russian male teenager had less chance of surviving to age sixty than his great-grandfather did in 1900. In effect, in certain key areas the Yeltsin government (with U.S. support) had cost Russia decades of social development.[8]

In assessing this period, Russia's distinguished historian Roy Medvedev has evaluated Boris Yeltsin's legacy as follows:

> There are no grounds for considering Boris Yeltsin among the great reformers of the twentieth century. . . . True, he assumed power in 1991 under bad conditions but he left the country in much worse shape when he resigned in 1999. The standard of living of the overwhelming majority of the population declined by 40-50% in these eight years and the number of people reduced to life at the margins of survival approached half the Russian population. Death rates significantly exceeded birth rates, leading to a reduction in the population of three million. Crime increased while the educational system, health system and state of culture virtually collapsed. . . .
>
> The evaporation of citizens' life savings, the destruction of the parliament by tank shot [in 1993], the [lost] war in Chechnya, the sale or simply giving away of the oil industry, banks, television stations, steel factories, etc., . . . are typical not of periods of development but of collapse and chaos.[9]

This domestic context of virtual anarchy framed all of the key choices that Putin would have to make once he became prime minister in August 1999. This chaos had its counterpart in foreign affairs as well.

FOREIGN POLICY RETREAT AND HUMILIATION

To many Russians, especially among the country's foreign policy and national security elites, Russia's international position also seemed to be collapsing. At the outset of Russia's post-Soviet course in 1992, the Russian government pursued a foreign policy that built upon Mikhail Gorbachev's revolutionary accomplishment in ending the Cold War. It sought to build a community of values with the advanced postindustrial democracies. According to President Yeltsin and young foreign minister Andrei Kozyrev, Russia's national interests were linked to its aspirations to build a free-market economy, nurture political pluralism, and join the international community of democratic states. This liberal internationalism had both a positive and a negative dimension. On the one hand, Russia would have to strive to become integrated into Western economic, political, and even security institutions. On the other hand, in this view Russia could not afford to alienate the West, lest exclusion from the international democratic community jeopardize Russia's own democratic prospects at home.

Almost immediately it became clear that there would be painful limits as well as payoffs to such an approach. While the United States did support Russia's demand that it be recognized as the chief successor state to the USSR and assume the Soviet seat on the UN Security Council, Russians generally found the foreign policy promise implicit in their country's liberal democratic aspirations wanting. American and West European economic aid packages, when stripped to their essentials, proved to be small fractions of the sums expected when both sides spoke of the need for a Marshall Plan for Russia. While it is doubtful whether more ambitious programs of aid could have made a decisive difference to Russia's post-Soviet economic trajectory, the discrepancy between Western promises and Western performance meant that the United States and Western Europe were blamed for Russia's failures. They promised much more than they could realistically achieve, and in the bargain Russians identified them with a cascading domestic calamity that they had not really initiated.

More than that, in their most important foreign policy decisions throughout the 1990s, the NATO states clearly indicated by their deeds that they would act on key issues of European security regardless of the Russian government's express concerns and reservations. Such disregard for Russian interests triggered a powerful backlash in Moscow against NATO and the United States in particular. Most traumatically, in March 1999, NATO initiated a three-month air war against Serbia–an informal Russian ally–over that government's human rights abuses in its province of Kosovo, culminating in June in the Serbians' loss of control over its cultural homeland. The Kosovo war in particular alarmed the Russian leadership and national security elites, as it was launched so soon after the first round of NATO expansion in May 1997. Although at that time Russia and NATO had signed a charter pledging each to detailed consultations involving security issues of mutual concern, the Kosovo war showed that such pledges were no obstacle to NATO taking action on its own, outside the UN Security Council (where Russia wielded a veto), and in flagrant disregard of Russian interests.

Although President Yeltsin had sent former prime minister Viktor Chernomyrdin to Belgrade to induce Serbian dictator Slobodan Milosevic to surrender, senior Russian military officers now undertook a rogue action. They cut off communications with the Russian Foreign Ministry and embassy in Belgrade; dispatched a force of paratroopers (on peacekeeping assignment in neighboring Bosnia) to seize an airfield in Pristina, Kosovo; and laid claim to a separate Russian peacekeeping zone in the province. In an operation that had the element of comic opera written all over it, the Russian force had been so hastily assembled that, having seized the airport, they had to beg approaching British troops for food and water. In the end, the Russians consented to a peacekeeping zone under NATO's aegis. Nonetheless, the episode underscored everything that had bedeviled Russian-Western relations since the breakup of the Soviet Union in 1991. Russia and the West wound up communicating with each other by armed deployments, as they had done so often during the Cold War. Indeed, the Russians were preparing to send an additional several thousand paratroopers to Kosovo. Only intense counterpressure by U.S. officials on the Bulgarian and Romanian governments to deny their airspace to Russian military aircraft foiled the Russians' plan.

In sum, vectors of force, rather than communities of shared values and interests, increasingly defined Russia's relations with the West in general, with NATO in particular, and above all with the United States. The experiences of the 1990s decisively altered Russia's initial liberal, internationalist assumptions about the essential harmony of Russian-Western relations. Consequently, Russia's foreign policy elites began to embrace the premises of political realism: Russia was alone in the world, no one would help it, and no one would pity it if it failed. Such views represented the mainstream consensus in the Russian foreign policy establishment in the mid- to late 1990s as Vladimir Putin made his way through the labyrinth of Kremlin politics all the way to the top.

SUMMONS TO MOSCOW

Putin resigned from St. Petersburg city hall in the early summer of 1996. Having failed to obtain a diplomatic appointment abroad, Putin was soon brought to Moscow by a St. Petersburg network already established in the capital. Putin had done local electoral work in 1995 and 1996 for Prime Minister Chernomyrdin's political party and then for President Yeltsin himself. Such services established Putin's modest but important reputation in Moscow.[10]

According to Putin, his former St. Petersburg colleague Aleksei Kudrin, then assistant director of the Presidential Administration (and later finance minister under Putin), initiated the move to bring Putin to Moscow. Kudrin was part of a small but tightly knit cell of St. Petersburgers working in the Krem-lin. In addition to Kudrin, this group included Aleksei Bolshakov, the deputy prime minister and a close associate of then prime minister Chernomyrdin, who for years was de facto capo of Gazprom, the post-Soviet Russian natural gas monopoly; the free-market economist Anatoly Chubais, designer of Rus-sia's ill-fated privatization program and another protégé of Sobchak's; Sergei Belyayev, chief of the pro-government parliamentary faction in the Russian Duma; and Alfred Kokh (later indicted in Switzerland on fraud charges), chief of the State Committee for Managing State Property.[11]

For the next three years, Russian politics were consumed by the struggle over who would succeed President Yeltsin with the presidential election sched-uled for the summer of 2000. The panic that Yeltsin's entourage had displayed throughout the Russian president's 1996 reelection campaign reflected the magnitude of the stakes that were involved. For the entire Yeltsin team, includ-ing Yeltsin and his family, the heart of the presidential succession problem was a question not just of transferring political power but also of securing their wealth, their freedom from imprisonment, and conceivably their lives.

Kremlin politics in this period was the byproduct of several strains of po-litical combat at the highest levels, the most important being that between free-market economic liberals, who at the time included Putin in their circle, and a group of wealthy, politically connected business oligarchs. These oligarchs, who included Yeltsin's financial adviser, Boris Berezovsky, were looking des-perately for ways to guarantee their newfound riches once Yeltsin would no longer be on the scene. Ultimately, it would be the logic of this winner-takes-all political maneuvering that would propel Putin to the Russian presidency.

One measure of the frantic instability of Kremlin politics during Putin's early years in Moscow is the fact that, between 1997 and 1999, President Yelt-sin fired and hired five prime ministers. In one instance, Yeltsin submitted the same candidate to the Duma three times, in effect daring the parliament to turn him down and risk a potentially violent confrontation, as had happened in the fall of 1993. Amid the Russian financial collapse of August 1998, for the post of prime minister the Duma compelled a now ailing Yeltsin to accept the appoint-ment of Yevgeny Primakov, who made no bones about the fact that he saw the wealth of Russia's post-Soviet oligarchs as illegitimate. For a time, Primakov's success in stabilizing the Russian economy after the economic crash made him the most likely successor to Yeltsin, a prospect that sent chills through Yeltsin's inner circle. And while Primakov himself would be fired in April 1999, in the months that followed he remained the focal point of Yeltsin's opposition and a highly plausible candidate to win the 2000 presidential election.

Putin's rise to the summit in Moscow between 1996 and 1999 reflected this dizzying pace of Kremlin politics. Having no independent foundation on which to assert a claim to national power, Putin reacted to events around him. In the process, Putin repeatedly proved himself to be an indispensable lieutenant and "enforcer" for his superiors, until he finally came to the attention of Boris Yeltsin himself.

His first Moscow assignment was as deputy to Pavel Borodin, director of the General Department of the Presidential Administration. Putin's brief included legal affairs, especially those related to Russian property held abroad, estimated at some $50 billion, in addition to another $600 billion throughout Russia itself.[12] (In 2001 U.S. authorities arrested Borodin and extradited him to Switzerland on international corruption charges. Putin was not implicated in the affair.) Putin managed to reorganize the department and introduce meaningful oversight of Kremlin property abroad. He now had new responsibilities but no real influence in Moscow. For the moment, he was on the side of the liberals against the oligarchs.

In March 1997 Putin was quickly made a deputy head of the Presidential Administration and chief of the main inspectorate of the Presidential Administration, which was the real locus of governmental authority in Russia. There he replaced his former St. Petersburg colleague Aleksei Kudrin, who was promoted by fellow St. Petersburger Anatoly Chubais to become deputy minister of finance. Chubais, a true free-market liberal, was impressed by Putin's Germanic work ethic and personal habits and saw the advantage of moving Putin into the heart of presidential power. Putin's job now was to ensure that President Yeltsin's decrees were actually carried out. Given the nature of Russian governance and the executive authority afforded the president's secretariat, this appointment made Putin more powerful than most government ministers.

Details of Putin's actions during this period are scarce. In his most delicate assignment, he had to complete an ongoing investigation of corruption charges against the Ministry of Defense, which Duma member Gen. Lev Rokhlin (Ret.) accused of illegally delivering $1 billion in weaponry free of charge to the Armenian government. Putin's report concluded that violations had occurred but that no documents implicated the former defense minister Pavel Grachev himself.[13] Overall, Putin evidently impressed Yeltsin with his businesslike manner, his mastery of the facts, his loyalty, and his discretion.

Putin was by now accustomed to the role of loyal and competent aide. He made a striking and positive impression on many who came into contact with him or observed him in action. Aleksei Venediktov, editor in chief of the independent radio station Ekho Moskvy, recalls, "When he did a live broadcast with me in 1997, I was surprised at how competent he was and well informed as to detail, which was generally not the case for Kremlin advisors in those days."[14] Putin himself claims to have been bored with administrative work, however high level, and even considered leaving the government. He later wrote, "I don't know what I would have done, if things had gone on like this. Most likely I would have established a law firm."[15]

In May 1998 Putin's superiors appointed him first deputy director of the Presidential Administration, with special responsibility for Russia's numerous federal regions. Putin now had true policy power and the opportunity to observe how chaotic and counterproductive Russia's patchwork federalism was, with its eighty-nine federal districts possessing varying degrees of autonomy, sovereignty, and even virtual independence of Moscow. Putin's chief duties in the less than three months that he held this office involved holding governors to account by monitoring how their regions spent the federal funds that Moscow allocated to them.

In July 1998, and in spite of his promise to Lyudmila never to return to intelligence work, Putin accepted the appointment as director of the FSB. Yeltsin offered to return him to active service with the rank of general, but Putin declined. Nevertheless, in his inaugural speech to the agency, Putin declared that he felt as if he "had returned home." In his capacity as FSB chief, Putin truly impressed Yeltsin as a capable and reliable subordinate, one perhaps able to secure the interests of Yeltsin and his "family" (both personal and political) during the uncertain succession that was due to take place within two years. Putin's successful handling of three tasks in particular seem to have persuaded Yeltsin and his entourage that Putin had the qualities needed in a trustworthy successor.

First, as Russia's spymaster, Putin immediately began purging the FSB of personnel considered disloyal to Yeltsin and his family. In less than a year, he fired fully one-third of the FSB's staff and reassigned countless others to distant

Putin was an active KGB officer from 1975 to 1990, serving as director of the Federal Security Bureau (FSB), successor agency to the KGB, in 1998–1999. Used by permission of the website of the President of the Russian Federation, www.kremlin.ru.

provinces.[16] Before Putin's arrival, the FSB had been the source of an endless stream of *kompromat* (compromising materials), or embarrassing information on audio and videotape, that were invariably aimed at Yeltsin's entourage. Under Putin, these leaks ceased altogether.

Putin then organized his own stunning kompromat campaign against Russia's chief prosecutor, Yuri Skuratov, who had been overheard on a bugged phone preparing indictments against Yeltsin's circle, including his daughter Tatyana. Putin had managed to catch Skuratov on film in flagrante delicto with two female prostitutes. He confronted Skuratov privately with this information in an effort to deter him from pursuing the indictments. When Skuratov later reneged, Putin had the films broadcast on Russian television, to the great shock of the Russian public, the disgrace of Skuratov (who suffered a heart attack), and the annulment of the indictments. Such pragmatic brutality endeared Putin to Yeltsin's closest advisers, who now saw that they could rely on him in a crisis.[17]

In March 1999, at a time when detailed operational plans were being drawn up for a new stage in the Russian-Chechen war (discussed in the following section), Putin became head of the National Security Council. He now controlled the levers of all of the power ministries in Russia, including the armed forces, the intelligence agencies, the police, border troops, customs, and tax police. Then, as we have already seen, Putin's dramatic and successful evacuation of his mentor, Anatoly Sobchak, from St. Petersburg to France in November 1998 added to his growing reputation for bold and decisive action. By mid-1999 Putin had earned Yeltsin's complete trust, with the Russian president assuming a somewhat paternal attitude toward his eventual successor. In Yeltsin's eyes, Putin seemed to have almost ideal qualities as his successor: Putin was clearly obligated to Yeltsin for his rapid rise, he didn't have his own team or financial resources (which could allow him to contest Yeltsin's entourage over the terms and aftermath of succession), and while Putin's background lay in intelligence, he was not a tool of the FSB, which Yeltsin feared. To close the deal, Putin had clearly demonstrated the ability to protect Yeltsin and his family once the latter was no longer president of Russia.[18] Soon, Putin would be prime minister.

THE CHECHEN CAULDRON

The challenges in Chechnya were daunting. Yeltsin's government had launched and lost a war in 1994 to bring the rebellious province back into the Russian fold. In the process, the incompetence and corruption of the Russian government had been revealed in striking terms. A remarkably free press and television campaign presented the war to a disgusted Russian public more as a clash between corrupt and criminalized elites in Moscow and Grozny than as a matter of Russia's vital national interests. A cease-fire organized just in time for the 1996 presidential election confirmed Russia's failure to subdue the Chechen move toward independence. For the next three years, not a single Russian soldier, police officer, court official, or tax collector operated in Chechnya, where Islamic sharia law prevailed. All the while, Chechnya became submerged ever deeper in the mire of drug running, narcotics and arms trafficking, counterfeiting, and kidnapping of foreigners for ransom. Russia did not invest a kopek for the reconstruction of the province, while Chechen criminal clans organized themselves with alarming impunity throughout Russia's major cities, including Moscow. Chechnya became plainly ungovernable, a festering sore not only to Russia but also to the broader international community.

After more than a year of small-scale attacks, bombings, and kidnappings, at the beginning of August 1999 a force of some two thousand Chechen guerrillas invaded the neighboring Russian province of Dagestan. The Chechens' declared aim–to establish an independent Islamic republic–no doubt was intended to persuade the Russian authorities of the futility of reclaiming Chechnya. This invasion proved to be the specific precursor to the second Russian-Chechen war of the 1990s and to the appointment of Vladimir Putin as Russia's prime minister. Yeltsin wanted someone tough to deal with this new Chechen challenge; he thus turned to Putin.

In early August 1999, Yeltsin broached the nomination of Putin with his chief of staff, Aleksandr Voloshin. For Yeltsin, the only question was when to do it: August, September, or October? Yeltsin liked the idea of early August, as most of official Russia would then be on vacation. Kremlin officials and the Duma would have three weeks or more to acclimate themselves to a choice they could not likely undo.

Yeltsin met with Putin on August 5, informing him that he would be appointed prime minister. Yeltsin also expressed his hope that Putin would buttress the efforts of pro-government forces in the December 1999 parliamentary elections. Putin, aware that he was at the time a political nonentity, was skeptical. He also told Yeltsin candidly that, in light of his experience in the 1996 St. Petersburg elections, he preferred to have nothing to do with them.

"And on whom are we going to rely in the elections?" asked Putin.

"I don't know," replied Yeltsin. "We'll build a new party. For you the main thing is to work in the government."

Then Yeltsin teased, "And what about the highest post of all [that is, the presidency]?"

Putin said, "I don't know, Boris Nikolayevich. I don't think that I'm ready for it."

Yeltsin, concluding: "Think about it. I believe in you."[19]

Putin's appointment was met with dismay and even opposition among Yeltsin's circle and throughout Russia's political class. Anatoly Chubais actively opposed the nomination and tried to dissuade Yeltsin from it. Chubais even turned to Putin directly, stating that it was better to refuse the assignment now of his own accord than to be forced out later by circumstances. Putin replied that he was at the president's disposal.

Yeltsin quickly advanced the nomination, which needed the Duma's approval. Prominent politicians from left to right dismissed the nomination as "absurd" (Moscow mayor Yury Luzhkov), "insane" (liberal democrat Boris

Nemtsov), "psychotic" (Communist Party leader Gennady Zyuganov), and, least insulting, "a technician for a government of technicians" (Vladimir Ryzhkov).[20] Nevertheless, the parliament, noted for receiving massive payoffs from off-budget funds in the Presidential Administration, held brief and anticlimactic hearings. The members approved Putin's nomination by a vote of 233 to 84, with 17 abstentions.[21]

In the space of just two years, Vladimir Putin had moved from one leading Kremlin position to another, winding up as head of the government. By the end of the year, he would be acting president and would soon be elected president for his own four-year term. Putin suddenly emerged as the historic and potentially heroic figure that he had dreamed of becoming while an impressionable teenager, fantasizing about a career of intrigue and derring-do. After more than two decades as a subaltern, albeit one whose obvious administrative talents became valued at ever-higher levels of the Russian government, Putin was now prime minister of Russia, still the world's second nuclear power. What would he make of this unexpected windfall of power?

4

PUTIN AT THE HELM
(1999–2000)

"The power ministries have no reason to organize a coup d'état.
For what? To take power? We have it already. To overthrow Yelt-
sin? This doesn't make sense, since it was he who appointed us."
— *Vladimir Putin, July 7, 1999*[1]

While Vladimir Putin would stake his political career on the war in
Chechnya, Putin inherited this war when he became prime minister on August
9, 1999. As noted, at the beginning of the month, about two thousand Chechen
guerrillas had infiltrated Chechnya's neighboring province of Dagestan in the
Russian Federation and declared that they wanted to establish an Islamic republic and ignite a broader conflagration throughout the Russian Caucasus.
Had Putin failed to meet this patent challenge to Russia's territorial integrity,
there is little doubt that he would have been cast aside just as countless previous prime ministers had been. More troubling, large parts of southern Russia
would have been transformed into essentially lawless zones susceptible to the
most radical Wahhabi Islamic fundamentalists, with implications not only for
Russia's remaining Muslim population—nearly 20 percent of the total—but for
international order as well. While the Russian government was prepared to
escalate the conflict with Chechnya, it was Putin and Putin alone who took the
risky decision to go beyond the existing plans to contain violence in the rebellious province and eradicate it at the source.[2]

Putin requested and received from President Yeltsin dictatorial powers
to conduct military operations in the North Caucasus.[3] Unlike his predeces-

sor, Viktor Chernomyrdin, and unlike Yeltsin himself during the first Russo-Chechen war, Putin took direct and public responsibility for the conduct of the war.[4] He faced two urgent tasks: defeating the Chechen guerrilla invasion of Dagestan and then, much more problematically, crushing the armed Chechen secessionist rebellion in Chechnya itself.

The first challenge proved simpler than many imagined at the time. In invading Dagestan, from which Russian troops had withdrawn the previous fall, the Chechen forces had overextended themselves. A complex and multiethnic province, Dagestani elites were much more Russified and resistant to radical Islam than their counterparts in Chechnya were. The local Dagestani government invited Russia to send troops to the province. A Russian force of ten thousand soldiers, in cooperation with Dagestani authorities and much of the civil population, quickly annihilated what amounted to a small foreign force. This victory paid an immediate dividend: Dagestan now became a base of support for Russian military actions in Chechnya.

Putin's initial reaction to the Dagestan crisis was set in motion by his predecessor, Sergei Stepashin, who had devised a contingency plan the previous spring in the event that the Russian-Chechen conflict escalated. The plan called for a large-scale military campaign against Chechnya but with carefully limited objectives. The goal was to establish a containment belt around the piedmont of the northern slope of the Caucasus Mountains, the most unstable and dangerous parts of Chechnya. Following the defeat of Chechen forces in Dagestan, stage one called for a large-scale Russian force to expel rebel forces from the northern plains of Chechnya and secure the frontier. Stage two would entail a systematic air campaign designed to reduce Chechen forces while limiting casualties to Russian ground troops. In stage three, Russian forces would push deeper into Chechnya and form a buffer zone on the northern bank of the Terek River. This move would bring key oil pipelines under Russian control. Russia would then try to persuade the majority of the Chechens, exhausted by years of war and chaos, that their lot was best cast with Russia. Russia, however, would not attempt to conquer all of Chechnya or storm the capital, Grozny. Instead, the Russians would seek to employ economic and political leverage to complement their military actions.[5] Putin pursued this established strategy from the time he assumed the premiership until mid-October 1999.

TERROR IN MOSCOW AND BEYOND

Russia's large-scale and decisive military reaction to the invasion of Dagestan undermined Chechen assumptions that they could sap Russia's will to maintain its authority in the North Caucasus. The Chechens then escalated their attacks. On September 4, 1999, they detonated a car bomb in front of an apartment building housing Russian soldiers' families in Buinaksk, Dagestan, causing 64 deaths and wounding another 66. Then, during the early morning of September 9, an unusually powerful explosion of more than 650 pounds of military-grade explosives leveled an eight-story apartment building on Guryanov Street in southeastern Moscow: 94 people were killed and 150 wounded. Four days later, on September 13, Chechen terrorists blew up a second Moscow apartment building, this one on Kashirskoye Boulevard, killing another 130 people, including 6 children, and wounding 150. On September 16, another bomb exploded outside an apartment building in Volgodonsk in southern Russia, killing 17 and wounding 480. In all, the four attacks killed 305 Russians and wounded 846 more.[6]

As anyone who was living in the United States on September 11, 2001, can easily imagine, four such bombings in short order, including two in Russia's capital, had a traumatic and decisive impact on the nation's political psychology. Overnight, Russians transformed their view of the situation in Chechnya. Whereas many had seen the first Chechen war (1994–1996) as a conflict between the corrupt and criminalized elites in Moscow and Grozny, most Russians now viewed the issue as a matter of vital interest to the Russian nation. Citizens' vigilante committees sprang up overnight. In a foretaste of abuses to come, the Russian authorities, with the public's approval, arbitrarily rounded up Chechens, or often anyone with swarthy features.

Putin pledged to do everything in his power to punish those responsible for the atrocities and to end the Chechen problem once and for all. By the time of the bombings, the Chechen guerrillas had been rousted from Dagestan and Russian troops partially occupied Chechnya in accord with the spring 1999 plan. After a month of intensive and often indiscriminate aerial bombardment, Putin launched the ground campaign in earnest in early October. By mid-October, he had achieved all of the key objectives of the operational plan that he had inherited: the Russian Army occupied Chechnya north of the Terek River, and the border was sealed. Chechen forces suffered heavy losses; Russian losses, by contrast, were light, reflecting their widespread use of airpower and heavy artillery. Many Russian observers expected an armistice might be arranged with the nominal Chechen head of state, Aslan Maskhadov.

It did not happen. Instead, Putin accepted a plan for total war presented by Armed Forces Chief of Staff Gen. Anatoly Kvashnin. Pointing to the implications of the September bombings, Putin justified his choice: "I was convinced that if we did not stop the extremists then and there, immediately, it would lead to a Yugoslav-type situation throughout the territory of the Russian Federation."[7]

The decision to "go to the source" was Putin's alone (Yeltsin had given him carte blanche on Chechnya). Many of his national security advisers and military leaders urged him to do otherwise. At the end of August, Putin convened a meeting with post-Soviet prime ministers Viktor Chernomyrdin, Sergei Kirilenko, Yevgeny Primakov, and Sergei Stepashin on the Chechnya problem. Not one of them advocated large-scale combat operations in the rebel province.[8] But Putin did.

The new prime minister reaped huge political dividends from extending the war in Chechnya. Putin's popularity soared, rising from 1 percent after Yeltsin nominated him to head the government to 16 percent after the four bombings in September, to 32 percent by the end of November, and more than 50 percent by the end of the year.[9] Suddenly, Putin became a plausible candidate for president. His words and deeds impressed a Russian nation desperately yearning for order and seeking a strong hand at the helm. Putin exercised charismatic leadership to large swaths of Russian society even if he alarmed and baffled Western and Russian liberals alike. If his rise to head the government was in many respects accidental, he now had become the most formidable figure in Russian politics.

Some of his critics, such as ex-oligarch Boris Berezovsky and the FSB defector Alexander Litvinenko, charged that Putin orchestrated the bombings in order to enhance his popularity as a candidate for the Russian presidency.[10] Berezovsky advanced these claims, however, only after Putin seized his television stations and drove him out of the country for criticizing the government's handling of the *Kursk* disaster in August 2000. Berezovsky's allegations are based on tendentious speculation and are not persuasive in light of some basic facts.

In the first place, the terror bombings in September 1999 followed a model employed by Chechen agents in southern Russia on two occasions the previous spring. Moreover, Chechen commander Ibn al-Khattab actually claimed responsibility for the atrocities. He later retracted it when he saw the catalytic effect the bombings had on the will of the Russian government and people to crush the Chechen rebellion once and for all.[11] Nor was there reason for Putin to believe that escalating the war in Chechnya would nurture his legitimacy in the eyes of the nation. On the contrary, the history of the first Chechen war and the hesitation of most Russian political leaders to reenter the conflict suggested that a war in Chechnya was a political dead end. As Chairman of the Duma Gennady Seleznev told Putin shortly after his nomination, "But what have [your political opponents] done to you? Haven't they buried you?"[12] Putin himself expected that waging war in Chechnya would likely cost him his political career. "This," Putin has said, "was a small price to pay and I was ready to pay it."[13] Indeed, he was astonished that his public approval ratings rapidly improved following the onset of large-scale combat operations in Chechnya.[14]

Finally, Putin did not need the bombings to justify his invasion and occupation of Chechnya. In response to the Chechen incursion into Dagestan, he was already implementing the spring 1999 war plan when the bombings occurred. He successfully completed the mission in mid-October, and there is no reason to think that he would not have carried out the plan without the bombings of the four apartment buildings. The bombings simply persuaded Putin to extend an ongoing military campaign and adopt a policy of total war against the Chechen rebellion.

TOTAL WAR

By December 1999, the Russian Army, now amounting to 150,000 troops versus some 20,000 Chechen guerrillas, occupied 60 percent of Chechnya and encircled the Chechen capital, Grozny. It crossed the Terek River, on the way to the capital, practically without casualties. Then, in seeming revenge for the humiliation it had suffered in the first war, the Russian Army bombarded the city mercilessly, causing many civilian deaths and forcing hundreds of thousands of people to flee the region. Satellite photographs subsequently showed that the center of Grozny had been razed. Russian television viewers saw little of the devastation or of the Russian military establishment's countless other crimes, as the government strictly limited press coverage of the war.

By the end of January, the Chechens' military situation in Grozny became untenable. During a desperate breakout operation launched by Chechen commander Shamil Basaev, the Russian Army annihilated the bulk of his 3,000-

Civilians come back to the main market in Grozny, Chechnya, the day after its destruction by a Russian missile (October 21, 1999). Antoine Gyori/Sygma/Corbis

man force in a fierce three-day battle. By late winter, the Russians had taken effective control of the Chechen capital. While the Russians then extended the campaign to the Chechen piedmont and mountains in the south, by the spring of 2000 they had destroyed the capacity of the Chechen side to undertake large-scale combat operations. To the large majority of Russians, it seemed that Putin had won in Chechnya where Yeltsin had lost.

PUTIN'S POLITICAL ASCENT

Most Russians had little sympathy for tales of Chechen suffering after the four September terror bombings. Putin made plain that he understood this psychology when he told the nation that he would "wipe out the Chechen thugs wherever they are, right up to the last shithouse."[15] Russian opinion united behind the government as never before, and Putin's standing grew rapidly with each successive stage of the Chechen war. The newly established pro-government Unity Party quickly morphed into the "Putin Party," cashing in on the premier's growing charismatic support. In a surprisingly effective parliamentary campaign, Putin deployed all of the financial, administrative, media, and police powers at his disposal in order to shape the outcome of the December elections to the Duma. He took no chances and spared no expense. In a particularly egregious abuse of media power, Boris Berezovsky's television station–at the time, Berezovsky was backing Putin at all costs–broadcast a graphic film of a heart operation on a patient alleged to be ex-premier Yevgeny Primakov. The object was to discredit Primakov, who was undergoing a serious operation in Switzerland and was the most plausible of Putin's rivals for president.[16]

In a detailed report on the December parliamentary elections, international observers documented the Russian government's systematic abuses of the electoral process. Executive authorities–governors, mayors, and so on–had interfered with the electoral process. They prevented opposition candidates from holding public meetings, threatened to fire political foes from their jobs, and arranged lopsided media coverage in favor of pro-government candidates. They encouraged military personnel to vote in favor of the pro-Kremlin Unity Party, and they used the government-controlled national television to denigrate and defame leading opposition candidates while lavishing attention and praise upon Putin and his Unity Party.

Moreover, amid the second Russo-Chechen war, antigovernment views were easily portrayed as antipatriotic and even treasonous. One presidential hopeful who dared to express even mild dissent from the official line on the Chechen war, the liberal economist Grigory Yavlinsky, saw his public support plummet. The Russian armed forces in Chechnya often displayed wanton brutality, which was documented at the time by the UN Human Rights Commission as well as by such courageous Russian journalists as Andrei Babitsky and Anna Politkovskaya, but this had no appreciable effect on the Russian public. Russians felt their vital interests were at stake and, as in the United States in the immediate aftermath of 9/11, gave the government every benefit of the doubt.

The pro-government Unity Party scored far better in the December 1999 elections than anyone had imagined at the time of its creation in late September. Unity, which was devoid of ideas except to support Putin, obtained 23 percent of votes cast, just behind the Communists at 24 percent. The bloc Fatherland–All Russia, which had been expected to sweep the elections on the road to the presidency, was far behind and no longer a serious contender for national power. Together with a large number of independent candidates and after forging alliances with smaller parties in the Duma, Unity was able to form a pro-government majority in the parliament for the first time since the early 1990s. All in all, and in spite of electoral abuses, the election results endorsed the course that Vladimir Putin had set for Russia.

YELTSIN ANOINTS PUTIN

The succession scenario that had obsessed Yeltsin and his entourage for the past few years began to take concrete form. In December 1999 Putin enjoyed popular approval ratings of greater than 50 percent for the first time. Clearly he could now be elected president in a competitive political environment. Yeltsin then took the last in a series of bold and fateful decisions that had been the hallmark of his presidency. On New Year's Eve 1999, he addressed the Russian nation on television and announced that he was resigning, effective immediately. According to the Russian Constitution, power then gravitated to the prime minister, Vladimir Putin, who became acting president pending new elections. Poignantly, Yeltsin apologized to the nation for having failed to keep his promise to organize a quick transition to peace, prosperity, and stability. He conceded that his role had been destructive rather than constructive. Telling the nation, "I [have] done the main job of my life. Russia will never return to the past," Yeltsin then asked forgiveness

> for not fulfilling some high hopes of those people who believed we would be able to jump from the grey, stagnating, totalitarian past into a bright, rich and civilized future in one go. I myself believed in this. But it could not be done at a stroke. In some respects I was too naïve. Some of the problems were too complex. We struggled on through mistakes and failures.[17]

The decision to step down in favor of Putin was Yeltsin's alone. Seeking no one's counsel, he had confided to Putin on December 14, 1999, that he was going to resign. Putin had tried to dissuade him, telling Yeltsin, "I don't think that I'm ready for this decision, Boris Nikolayevich. Don't you see . . . that this would be a rather heavy burden. It's very important that we continue to work together. Mightn't it be better for you to leave office as scheduled [in the coming summer]?"[18]

Yeltsin nonetheless had insisted and Putin agreed to succeed him. A fortnight would pass, however, before Yeltsin told Putin about the timing of his move. On the morning of December 29, Yeltsin invited Putin into his office and said the transfer of power would take place two days later. The element of surprise was reinforced by the fact that the previous day Yeltsin had recorded a customary address to be broadcast to the nation on New Year's Eve. Only then did Yeltsin confide to his chief aides that he was leaving. And he waited until the morning of New Year's Eve itself to tell his wife the impending news. Mere hours later he broadcast it to an amazed nation, which had a new president by noon, January 1, 2000. Formally, Yeltsin's decision–followed as it was by a nationwide election–affirmed the principle that political succession in Russia should be a rule-governed transition rather than an ad hoc and necessarily ad hominem affair. In practice, though, the transfer had more to do with the logic of court interests and intrigue than settled constitutional procedure.

On the eve of his ascension to the presidency, Putin published a statement known as the Millennium Manifesto, in which he set forth his vision of Russia's challenges and future. He embraced Russia's Christian cultural legacy and emphatically criticized Soviet communism for having led Russia through a "blind alley" of seven decades of stunted economic and social development and isolation from world affairs. Declaring the time of upheavals to be over, Putin stated that Russia needed to define its own path in the twenty-first century, one neither copied blindly from the West nor based on nostalgia for the Soviet past. While there should be no officially imposed state ideology, Russian society should be infused with the spirit of patriotism. Russia, Putin said, remained a great power in world affairs and should strive to establish a strong state at home that would be able to manage a mixed economy effectively. Underscoring the length of the road ahead, Putin noted that if Russia sustained fifteen consecutive years of economic growth at 8 percent per year, it would attain the present per capita GDP of Portugal, then the poorest country in Western Europe. In many respects, Putin's manifesto reflected a sophisticated, if abstract, understanding of the impact of the Soviet legacy on Russia's postcommunist future. The years to come would reveal how Putin would seek to balance the requirements of a modern, dynamic, and fluid society with the prerogatives of the strong state that he was equally determined to build.[19]

PRESIDENT PUTIN

The first decree that Putin signed, on the very day that he assumed the presidency, dealt with the living conditions of Boris Yeltsin and his family in retirement. Among other items, the decree provided for the complete immunity from prosecution of Yeltsin and his immediate family for all acts committed during his presidency, thereby satisfying Yeltsin's central interest in exchange for abiding by constitutional rules. In this way, Putin accomplished for Yeltsin what U.S. president Gerald Ford did for Richard Nixon with his preemptive presidential pardon in 1974. In dispensing an act of mercy, each leader sought to spare his country the agony of a prolonged settling of accounts with a divisive and disgraced president. No doubt there was also an element of quid pro quo in Putin's action.

Putin then briefly addressed the Russian people in his own New Year's address. He sought to reassure the nation about the continuity of government after Yeltsin's surprise resignation. Stressing that there would not be a "vacuum of power" in Russia "for even one minute," Putin promised that the Russian Constitution would continue to be respected. He pledged,

> The freedom of speech, freedom of conscience, the freedom of the mass media, the rights of private property—these fundamental elements of a civilized society—will be reliably protected by the state. The Armed Forces, the border troops and the police will carry out their work as before. The state has stood and will continue to stand in defense of every Russian person.[20]

That evening, Putin flew with his wife, Lyudmila, to celebrate the advent of the New Year and the new millennium not in St. Petersburg (as originally planned) but in Chechnya. The war there would absorb the lion's share of Putin's presidency in the years to come.[21]

Yeltsin's resignation triggered a constitutional clause stipulating that, in the event of the president's resignation or death, new elections would be held in three months' time, that is, by March 2000 instead of June. Yeltsin's move thus deprived the opposition of three months' campaigning time and presented an enormous tactical advantage for Putin, who could deploy all of the trappings of incumbency, including the formidable symbolism of chief of state, to his electoral advantage. Caught completely unawares by Yeltsin's dramatic transfer of power, Putin's political foes conducted a perfunctory campaign. The Russian presidential election, now scheduled for March 26, 2000, became anticlimactic.

Putin unquestionably had the support of the military, intelligence, and national security elites, as well as virtually all of the financial oligarchs, including his later nemesis Boris Berezovsky. The government's impressive apparatus as well as the government-controlled and pro-government private mass media (themselves controlled by oligarchs like Berezovsky) severely limited the reach of the opposition candidates' messages. At the same time, the course of events in the fall of 1999 showed that Putin drew increasing support from broad sectors of Russian society that desperately wanted order, stability, and an end to the Chechen rebellion. Even Putin's severest critics agree that his actions corresponded to this yearning for stability and strong leadership.[22]

Putin was fortunate in his opponents. The most prominent among them was the Communist Party, which was technically the winner in the December 1999 Duma elections but was unable to form alliances to establish a government. Indeed, the communists had support, especially among older voters, that was solid but difficult to expand beyond 25–30 percent of the electorate. It was essentially a reactionary party in a society that could not possibly revert to Soviet times. The Communist Party's effort to identify Putin with Yeltsin simply did not connect with most Russians, who were impressed by his youth, vigor, competence, and decisiveness. All of these traits stood in glaring contrast to the departed and pathetic Yeltsin. Indeed, Putin's popularity rating jumped in the weeks after Yeltsin's departure. In a series of major independent polls, the percentage of Russian voters who approved of Putin jumped to 77 percent by the end of January 2000.[23]

Putin's official inauguration as president of Russia (May 7, 2000). With outgoing Russian President Boris N. Yeltsin, Moscow. Antoine Gyori/Sygma/Corbis

Russian liberals criticized Putin as a looming Russian Augusto Pinochet, or dictator. But this depiction of Putin as a strong man worked in his favor, especially as it came from a liberal camp whose policies had been thoroughly discredited throughout the past decade. Putin himself "campaigned" without a program, confident that he would remain the most popular candidate. He cast himself as a leader above party politics and a president of all the people. In an eleven-candidate race with a turnout of 68 percent of the eligible voters, Putin won 52.9 percent of the vote, an impressive outcome anywhere in multicandidate elections. Gennady Zyuganov, the Communist Party candidate, came in second with 29.2 percent of the vote, while third place went to the free-market economist Grigory Yavlinsky, whose showing at just 5.8 percent augured poorly for the Russian liberals' prospects in the years ahead. In a hopeful sign of electoral maturity, the national chauvinist Vladimir Zhirinovsky, whose misnamed Liberal Democratic Party of Russia had garnered 24 percent of the vote in the December 1993 elections, received negligible support at less than 3 percent.[24]

The Putin era now began in earnest.

5
PUTIN IN POWER:
DOMESTIC POLITICS AND POLICIES

"Boys, the Duma is under no circumstances the place to be
talking politics."
*—Boris Gryzlov, head of the United Russia faction in the Russian
Duma and an old Putin hand from St. Petersburg, 2005*[1]

Suppressing the Chechen rebellion, as urgent as it was, was just one
among a multitude of serious challenges facing Putin's Russia. Russia at the
turn of the twenty-first century was still staggering under the impact of the Soviet collapse and the failed economic and social policies of the Yeltsin period.
Decline at home and retreat abroad seemed to many thoughtful observers to
call into question the future of Russia itself. And while there was broad agreement among Russia's political elites that Russia should count as a great international power, it was also clear that without economic recovery at home and
the revival of the state's capacity to govern, the country would matter little in
world politics.

Moreover, as Putin declared early in his administration, the main purpose
of Russian foreign policy now was to aid in the development of a truly modern economy and society. As he put it in his 2001 State of the Nation address,
"Foreign policy is both a reflection of and an essential factor in internal affairs.
Russia's economic situation depends on how competently we exploit our diplomatic resources."[2] In turn, Russia's international standing would depend on
the health of the economy and the related stability of the state and its society.

At the outset of his presidency, Putin pursued policies that had the support of many Russian liberals as well as nationalists in the military and intelligence bureaucracies. Even early critics conceded that he appealed to the Russian population's deeply rooted longing for order and stability after the chaos of the Yeltsin and Gorbachev years. Having crushed the organized Chechen military resistance by the spring of 2000, Putin then turned to a series of economic reforms aimed at lowering taxes and unleashing entrepreneurial energy in the agricultural and industrial sectors.

Before he could build on these developments, the sinking of the nuclear submarine *Kursk* in August 2000 unleashed a torrent of hostile media coverage that taught Putin it was more important to punish the messenger than deal with the root institutional causes of the catastrophe. From this point on, Putin resolved the tensions between the freedoms required for a dynamic, modern society and the control needed for an authoritative public order increasingly in favor of the latter. The methods by which he built his power base, with their heavy reliance on state control of huge swaths of the economy and society, foreclosed the development of meaningful democratic or even legal governmental accountability. Had Putin saved the Russian state at the expense of the free development of Russian society? Whether it was in terms of state capitalism and a related tsunami of corruption, strict government control of televised political news, blatant political manipulation of the judicial system, harassment of political opponents, or studied indifference to the murder of a score of critical journalists, Putin in two terms as president had created a political machine that, in spite of its undeniable stability, seemed incapable of genuine evolution.

PUTIN SETS HIS COURSE

As is true with any leader, Putin's initial political challenge was to establish his authority to govern. This task was complicated by the obvious fact that, without Boris Yeltsin's blessing, Putin could never have become president of Russia. Putin entertained no illusions about this point, as evidenced by his first presidential act: he granted Yeltsin and his family immunity from prosecution. Putin's conduct in his early years in office indicates that other "understandings" governed his presidential transition. First, he kept in place the main figures in the Russian Presidential Administration, all of whom were Yeltsin's protégés: Aleksandr Voloshin, Vladislav Surkov, Sergei Prikhodko, and Dzhakhan Pollyeva, among others. Moreover, Putin kicked upstairs to honorific posts Yeltsin's daughter Tatyana and her husband, Valentin Yumashev, even while extending presidential immunity to them.[3] To be sure, Putin began to staff the administration with loyalists mainly from his days in Sobchak's administration in St. Petersburg, including his eventual choice as presidential successor, Dmitri Medvedev. Still, as he made clear in his inaugural presidential address to the Russian National Security Council, "Everyone should continue to work where they are." Continuity with the Yeltsin team was the watchword, at least at the outset.

Yeltsin appears to have reached additional agreements with Putin. Basic continuity in the Presidential Administration would extend to government operations. While Putin appointed two colleagues from St. Petersburg days to key economic posts—the liberal economist German Gref, who was responsible for economic development, and Aleksei Kudrin as finance minister—it was Yeltsin who proposed that Mikhail Kasyanov should be Putin's successor as prime minister, a post Kasyanov held for the next four years. Otherwise, the government remained largely as it was when Yeltsin appointed Putin prime minister in early August 1999. There was no doubt an element of prudence in this continuity insofar as Putin did not yet have a team of advisers experienced in public administration at the highest levels. Over time this situation would change.

For his part, Yeltsin evidently pledged not to criticize Putin publicly and, in exchange, was able to retire in peace and comfort and with official respect as "the first president of Russia." In turn, Putin promised not to criticize Yeltsin's record as president or that of his government, a commitment that he kept. Notwithstanding the deplorable conditions into which Russia had fallen in the 1990s, Putin never blamed Yeltsin. In addition, judging by his inaugural speech to the nation as president and his subsequent performance, Putin likely agreed not to change the Russian Constitution, which was Yeltsin's creation. Thus, Putin declared on New Year's Eve 1999, "I wish to emphasize that any attempt to go beyond the framework of Russian law or the Constitution will be decisively stopped."[4] So long as Yeltsin was alive, Putin was as good as his word. Finally, Putin retained Anatoly Chubais as chairman of Russia's national electric power monopoly. Chubais had ferociously opposed Yeltsin's appointment of Putin both as prime minister and as presidential successor, so Chubais's continuation in a position of authority indicated that Yeltsin's entourage had influence in Putin's early administration.[5]

While Putin would achieve a certain measure of independence from Yeltsin's team once he had been elected president in March 2000, much of his first term was spent in its shadow. Over time, Putin gradually shifted the balance in his administration from Yeltsin to Putin loyalists, but as Kasyanov's four-year term as prime minister shows, it was a prolonged and often uncertain process. Initially, Putin had to build his network in Moscow; then he could expand it to the country at large.

Slowly but surely, Putin extended his grip over the reins of government. By 2003, he had appointed 70 percent of the key staff in the Presidential Administration. Toward the end of his second term as president in early 2008, Putin had appointed officials in more than 80 percent of the top 825 positions in the Russian government as a whole, while 80 percent of Russia's regional governors belonged to Putin's United Russia Party. Members of the military, intelligence, and security services held more than two-fifths of these top positions.[6] More broadly, the number of government bureaucrats increased by 66 percent in the later Putin years, from 527,000 to 878,000, absorbing 20 percent of the country's GDP. By 2010, Putin's appointees disposed of 40 percent of Russia's GDP through government spending.[7]

Apart from placing his people at the critical levers of power, Putin had to master what Russian journalist Vladimir Solovyov has called "a Kremlin with many towers."[8] The chief "towers," or constituencies, that Putin had to balance included

- a relatively small group of financial oligarchs who exercised often decisive influence on Russian politics for their personal interests throughout the 1990s;
- a substantial group of Yeltsin-era appointees that Putin had inherited and whose loyalties could never be taken for granted;
- a faithful group of civilian associates from St. Petersburg days, including free-market economists German Gref, Aleksei Kudrin, and Andrei Illarionov, as well as Putin's own successor, Dmitri Medvedev; and
- a second group of Putin loyalists from his personal contacts in the St. Petersburg intelligence agencies, the Federal Security Service, and the old Dresden branch of the KGB.

These intelligence officers, as well as military and other paramilitary personnel, came to constitute a major part of Putin's system of government when his second term began in 2004.[9] Throughout his tenure in high office, Putin was preoccupied with maintaining a balance among these factions that would both preserve his power and allow him to govern.

Stalin said famously that "personnel decide everything." In building his network of power, Putin inevitably chose individuals whose inclinations would shape the outcomes of his policy decisions. Putin understood from the start that Russia needed to establish the state's capacity to govern with reasonable effectiveness. Without more authoritative governmental institutions, he would not be able to catalyze the Russian economy or create a foundation for great-power status abroad.

But there seemed to be a major conflict in Putin's mind between the requirements of order, with its focus on command, and those of development, with its emphasis on the free evolution of society. Up to a point, such tension was inevitable and even creative. After all, without some minimum level of security—physical, economic, social, as well as territorial—it is difficult to see how a democratic society can function. This tension between order and development was clearly reflected in the makeup of his governing team and the thrust of its policies. During much of his first term (2000–2004), Putin's government made impressive progress in economic reform, passing major tax and property rights legislation while also asserting its authority over a fractured and dysfunctional system of public administration. By the middle of his second term, however, the very success that Putin enjoyed in reestablishing order and stability in Russia, enforced disproportionately by those with backgrounds in the military and intelligence sectors and who were suspicious of great wealth beyond the purview of the state, seemed increasingly to call into question Russia's future as a balanced economy and modern society. This remained the case despite an undeniable recovery of the economy and an improvement in Russians' living standards since 1999.

A series of specific events—the sinking of the nuclear submarine *Kursk* in August 2000, the appalling terrorist attacks in Moscow in 2002 and southern Russia in 2004, the ongoing war (albeit at a much lower intensity of fighting) in Chechnya, the possible spillover effects of the collapse of pro-Russian governments in Ukraine and Georgia, and a generalized insecurity at having to contest even nominally competitive elections—pushed the Russian government ever more decisively toward the pole of order. So long as the price of oil and natural gas, Russia's chief export commodities, stayed high (as they did through Putin's eight years as president), this tension between order and development could be managed with minimum political difficulty, and its long-term economic consequences could be disguised. It is a telling irony that, Chechnya aside, the first real test of Putin's presidency came when he was no longer chief of state and the world price of oil collapsed from $145 per barrel in July 2008 to less than $35 by the end of that year.

ECONOMIC PROGRAM

Early in his administration, Putin pushed a series of economic measures through the Duma: the first law allowing the buying and selling of land under market conditions, a reduction of capital gains taxes on foreign direct investment, a general reorganization of the tax code to simplify and lower taxes on business, as well as a single flat tax of 13 percent on personal income. Within the year, such measures produced a notable increase of tax revenues flowing into Russian state coffers. Even in the long-problematic agricultural sector, Putin's policies stimulated growth. Aggressive government intervention in the form of establishing a system of agricultural banks, price supports, countercyclical government intervention in commodities markets, and export tariffs helped to fuel a recovery. The value of total agricultural production attained 78 percent of the 1990 level, or double the average level of the post-Soviet 1990s. In 2008 Russian grain production was the highest in twenty years.[10]

Putin also made it clear that in spite of the massive fraud perpetrated on the Russian state during the privatization and loans-for-shares programs of the 1990s, he would not call into question the resulting redistribution of property through wholesale renationalization. So long as the oligarchs stayed out of politics and displayed some interest in using their assets for the country's economic development, Putin would stay out of their business affairs.

In the meantime, the Russian economy was beginning to grow for the first time in any sustained way in more than two decades. In fact, this development had begun before Putin assumed power, as the ruble's massive devaluation overnight in the August 1998 crash made much of Russian industry competitive on the Russian market against foreign imports. The price of oil was also on the rise and generating revenue, so by the time Putin took office as president in early 2000, the country was facing a favorable economic conjuncture.

For the next eight years, Russia enjoyed average growth rates of 7 percent per year. The country's GDP gradually recovered to the levels of 1990, and the average living standards of the population roughly doubled, compared to 1998. By the end of Putin's second presidential term, and for the first time in Russian history, a substantial portion of Russian society (perhaps as much as 25–30 percent) enjoyed a reasonably comfortable standard of living. Newly prosperous and dynamic major cities, such as Moscow and St. Petersburg, as well as significant provincial cities like Nizhny Novgorod, had become unrecognizable to anyone who had seen these locales in the 1990s or during the Soviet period. For large parts of the Russian population, Putin's first two terms were arguably the best period in Russian history.

While Putin was thus definitely the beneficiary of economic circumstances beyond his control, he was far from a simply passive collector and dispenser of fuel revenues. Beyond the set of integrated tax and property reforms that Putin undertook within his first year in office, in 2003 Putin accepted Finance Minister Kudrin's recommendation to establish an Oil Stabilization Fund, modeled on Norway's arrangement with Statoil, to exploit the advantages and minimize the disadvantages of the massive cash flow rolling in as a result of the steadily increasing world oil prices. This sophisticated and reasonably well-run project was specifically designed to build a financial shock absorber to insulate Russia from what economists have come to call the Dutch disease, after the Netherlands' experience upon discovering large natural gas deposits in the North Sea in the early 1960s.[11]

By siphoning a significant part of fuel export revenues into a state trust fund, the Russian government thereby dampened inflationary pressures, reduced the corresponding tendency to revaluation upward of the ruble (and thus cheapen imports, with negative effects on Russian producers), and squirreled away money for the day when world oil prices would come down. Upward of 90 percent of all oil export revenues above $27 per barrel went into this stabilization fund and other government coffers. By mid-2008, when oil hit $145 per barrel, this fund amounted to more than $150 billion, while the Russian Central Bank's international currency reserves amounted to $598 billion, or three times as much as Russia's dollar-denominated GDP when Putin took office in 1999.[12] By 2008, Russia possessed the third-largest quantity of foreign exchange reserves in the world, after Japan and China.

Putin also used energy revenues to establish Russia's creditworthiness. When he assumed office, Russia's foreign debt amounted to nearly 90 percent of Russian GDP; annual servicing of that debt absorbed one-quarter of the

Russian federal budget. This outlay severely constrained the policy options available to the government and underscored the country's dependence on Western creditors. The situation seemed so hopeless that in January 2001 trial balloons were being floated out of the Russian Presidential Administration that Russia had no choice but to repudiate its foreign sovereign debt or at least the substantial portion that it inherited from the defunct Soviet Union. Putin quickly rejected such talk once he saw the negative reaction in foreign markets and chancelleries. Russia could not afford to isolate itself from the world market; this move, Putin understood, was a central failing of the Soviet system. By 2005 the Russian government, now flush with energy revenues, paid off the country's entire foreign sovereign debt, even incurring a penalty of $1 billion for early repayment as the price for demonstrating both Russia's credit worthiness and its newfound independence of foreign creditor governments. The era of Russia's often-humiliating submission to the edicts of the International Monetary Fund was over.

Putin took further steps to ensure that the government would be solvent, even under worst-case scenarios involving a collapse in the price of oil. In striking contrast to the Yeltsin years, Putin insisted on and obtained budgets in the black, typically running a surplus of 4–7 percent of GDP. Russia's foreign trade, reflecting the exceptional place that fuel exports occupied in an era of rising world commodity prices, ran huge annual surpluses, while the world's leading credit-rating agencies upgraded Russian government securities to investment level.

Finally, in addition to the Oil Stabilization Fund, Putin established a special state investment fund designed to accumulate energy revenues. Its explicit purpose was to direct capital investment in the country's decrepit industrial, transportation, and communications infrastructure as well as in its human capital, and in the process Putin hoped to position Russia as a post–raw materials, postindustrial economy for the twenty-first century. Toward this end, in February 2008, Putin presented his initial 2020 program for economic renovation. Ironically, this program met strong resistance from many economists in Putin's government, including Finance Minister Kudrin. Massive short-term investment in infrastructure, they argued, would not only stimulate inflation but also achieve little, since much of it would be siphoned off in corrupt transactions. They maintained it would be much better to use such funds only for servicing the country's foreign debt.[13] As it turned out, these funds had to be used to buffer the economy during the emergency of 2008–2009, and significant direct investment in infrastructure has yet to take place. Still, the very establishment of such funds reflects the insight that Putin and his chief economic advisers shared that it would be dangerous in the long run for Russia to remain as dependent on the energy and raw materials sectors as it is today.

To be sure, much of Putin's economic success did rely on revenue from oil and natural gas exports, which accounted for nearly two-thirds of Russia's export receipts, half or more of the government's budget, and as much as thirty percent of the country's GDP.[14] Absent a move toward diversifying the Russian economy by increasing the share of agriculture, services, and knowledge-based industries in overall GDP, such dependency is potentially quite dangerous. Putin's Russia was running the risk of becoming a petrostate similar to Venezuela, where the combination of massive energy revenues and an authoritarian, nontransparent, and corrupt public administration tends to create a vicious circle of stunted economic and political development. Indeed, in 2010, Transparency International, a global monitoring group, ranked Russia tied with Venezuela (at 154 out of 178 countries evaluated) as one of the most corrupt societies on earth).[15]

In such an economy, the easy revenues to be had from the energy sector are invariably controlled by the government and strongly reduce the political incentives to diversify the foundations of economic growth and political support. The economy and the political system thus tend to grow ever more dependent on the energy sector over time. In addition, the government's relatively greater reliance on energy revenues instead of tax receipts reduces the incentive for the government to reach a social compact with its own citizens. The state's corresponding independence from society that ensues from this condition has the effect of reinforcing existing tendencies toward authoritarianism, nontransparent decision making, the "law of (informal) rules" over the rule of (formal and codified) law, and corruption.

The consequent narrowing of the government's constituency base means that when commodity prices eventually fall, the crisis that ensues will have a fateful political, as well as economic, dimension. As the government tends to spend most of the additional revenue obtained from high oil prices in order to satisfy key domestic clients and constituencies, it relies ever more on higher energy prices in a kind of ratcheting-up effect. Under Putin, plentiful energy revenues allowed the government to provide massive subsidies for domestic consumption of natural gas, to fund the war in Chechnya without drawing funds from social welfare commitments, to build up the country's dollar and euro reserves, and to pay off the country's sovereign debt. Over time, the government thus became more vulnerable to even modest drops in energy prices. In the event the price declined significantly over a prolonged period, the government would thus risk being thrown into real crisis. In this case, it would face the choice of negotiating a new political and social compact with society, entailing greater political democratization; engaging in much more repression than the highly selective kind that has been the case so far during the Putin years; or using remaining revenues to subsidize powerful political and social constituencies and buying short-term social peace at the expense of long-term economic development.[16]

In practice, the political economy that Putin constructed after his first several years in office increased rather than decreased the chances that Russia would confront such a fate. Step by step, often in response to unforeseen crises, Putin repeatedly concentrated power in the political, economic, and social systems and placed in positions of immense authority individuals who understood only the administrative control of people and things and not the organic functioning of a complex social system. Growing government domination of the energy sector also dramatically strengthened the grip of Putin's administration over Russian society, making possible the establishment of a distinctive political machine that combined authoritarian politics with democratic political forms.

In such a "corporatist" machine, bordering on kleptocracy, the group in power captures the state and the critical sources of revenue flow in the economy.[17] Once in place, the "machine" seeks to control or co-opt every major public institution in the country—political parties, election boards, courts, police, media—in an effort to obtain the benefits of electoral legitimacy without risking true political competition. Before the first year of his presidency had run its course, Putin had begun to build his own machine by reining in Russian television after a crisis that shook him to the core.

THE SINKING OF THE *KURSK*

On the morning of August 12, 2000, the Russian Northern Fleet lost contact with the nuclear-powered submarine *Kursk*, the most modern warship in the Russian Navy, while on exercise in the Barents Sea north of mainland European Russia. The 24,000-ton *Kursk* was armed with powerful torpedoes and cruise missiles, with the primary aim of sinking enemy (U.S.) aircraft carriers in wartime, and was capable of striking multiple surface targets simultaneously while submerged. The previous year the *Kursk* had made a successful voyage to the South Atlantic and Mediterranean, in the shadow of U.S. and NATO fleets; now, the Kursk had disappeared less than sixty miles from Russian shores. Northern Fleet command did not seem especially alarmed about the loss of contact, even though around noon signals officers reported two loud booming sounds emanating from the seafloor, one louder than the other. U.S. submarines monitoring the Russian exercises and Norwegian seismologists also picked up the sounds. Unquestionably, a massive explosion had occurred.

The Americans and Norwegians at once pinpointed the spot where the *Kursk* rested on the seabed. In fact, the Americans grasped the full magnitude of the accident twelve hours before Russian authorities did. Throughout the afternoon the Russian fleet commander attempted to make contact with the *Kursk* but without success. Late that evening the *Kursk* was declared damaged and the search for it began. It turned out that the submarine lay at a depth of about 350 feet, but the Russian Navy's rescue craft were unable to operate effectively in depths greater than 200 feet.

At 7 a.m. the next day, August 13, Russian defense minister Marshal Igor Sergeyev informed Putin about the accident. Sergeyev presented a sober but reassuring picture of the situation. The *Kursk* had food and water for a week, the atomic reactors had shut down automatically, and the ship was operating smoothly on reserve power. There were no dangerous radiation leaks, and in general the navy was on top of the situation. Detailed rescue plans for the crew's evacuation, should that prove necessary, had been worked out. Reassured, Putin decided not to change his plans for a five-day working holiday in Sochi, located in southern Russia on the Black Sea. He left the matter in the Russian military's hands.

Preliminary probes indicated that grave injury had been done to the *Kursk*: the nose of the vessel had been blown off, with much of the rest of the craft sustaining serious damage. It soon became clear, in the words of Adm. Vladimir Kuroyedov, that hopes for saving the submariners were "slim." Nevertheless, rescue efforts continued. Time and again, the Russians attempted to open the emergency hatch on the *Kursk* without success.

The Russian military command, in an operation then being widely and often sensationally covered in the Russian press and television, denied that it needed foreign assistance and rebuffed offers of help from the governments of Great Britain, Norway, and the United States.[18] Putin only asked for foreign assistance on August 15 or 16, after witnessing his people's outcry following the military's refusal of foreign assistance; but the request went through channels. In the meantime, Norwegian and British rescue teams had been busily preparing for just such an eventuality.

Shortly after midnight on August 19–or nearly eight days after the disaster– the foreign rescue teams arrived. In a stunning development that shocked much of Russian society, the Norwegians were able in twenty minutes to accomplish what had eluded the Russians for nearly a week: they gained access to the inside of the submarine. But any chance of rescuing the crew had long been lost.

For much of that week, meanwhile, Putin had remained on vacation in Sochi and Yalta. By deciding that there was nothing that he could do either in Moscow or on the scene to assist the rescue effort, Putin seemed to abdicate responsibility for the tragedy. The instinctive secrecy of the Russian military establishment and the bureaucracy in general fueled a conviction in Russian society that the government was either incompetent or indifferent to the sailors' predicament and their families' suffering.

Withering criticism placed Putin in a precarious situation. The impact of the *Kursk* disaster might be compared to that of the failed Bay of Pigs invasion of Cuba on the early John F. Kennedy administration, in the sense that each event had a formative influence on subsequent policies. But whereas Kennedy became more skeptical of the plans and premises of his military and intelligence advisers, Putin decided that it was more important to punish and control the media that had spread the bad news. While Putin would later admit–for the only time known to the author–that he was wrong on a matter of high policy,[19] he saw now how hostile media coverage could undermine the political foundations of his administration. He resolved to limit the independence of Russian national television networks.

Putin took aim at the media networks owned or controlled by the financial oligarchs Boris Berezovsky and Vladimir Gusinsky, who deployed their media assets in direct support of their general business and political interests. He drove Berezovsky out of the country on corruption charges and seized control of his television stations, which broadcast throughout Russia. Putin also orchestrated the takeover of Gusinsky's Media-Most empire by the state-controlled natural gas monopoly Gazprom. Gusinsky too would flee the country.[20] Putin thereby established a pattern that would only intensify in the years to come. National television was, in effect, much too important to leave out of the state's hands. As the Russian political scientist Lilia Shevtsova has observed,

> In the evolution of every leader there comes a time when he is tested, and those times decisively influence the way he thinks and force him to make choices that affect him forever after and constrain his room to maneuver. These tests establish or strengthen a particular vector in everything the governing authorities undertake. . . . Putin's first moment of truth came in August 2000 with the loss of the . . . *Kursk*. . . . His inaction throughout the tragedy elicited a storm of criticism from the then independent Russian media. The conclusion Putin evidently drew from this was that he needed to get rid of the independent mass media so that no one should again dare to impugn his leadership or suggest he was weak and unable to respond to challenges. If he had learned a different lesson from the *Kursk* tragedy, Russia just might have chosen a different path.[21]

There was almost certainly an important psychological dimension to Putin's media crackdown in the wake of the *Kursk* tragedy. He seems to have been overcome by a sense of helplessness when he lost control over these events. Undoubtedly this influenced his decision not to depart from his routine and take charge of the situation; there seemed to be little that Putin could have done operationally to influence the military's rescue operation. Moreover, as a career paramilitary officer, Putin was loath to interfere with professional military judgment. Such considerations, while understandable up to a point, overlooked his political role as the leader of Russian society and the mover of the bureaucracy.

From Putin's perspective, there could still be situations in which he was not only powerless but even endangered by the liberties and license of postcommunist Russian society. Fearing any loss of control appears to be a central element of Putin's psychological makeup. Exercising self-control through judo had taken young Putin off the streets, marked his amazing career, and helped him reach the highest post in the Kremlin. The vacuum of power that Putin had witnessed in Dresden in 1989 and then again in Russia throughout the 1990s underscored the dangers of ceding command over the apparatus of political power. The remarkable political machine that he built in two terms as Russian president, beginning with his assault on the media following the sinking of the *Kursk*, stands as impressive testimony to the strength, depth, and durability of Putin's fear of losing control over events and people.

HARNESSING THE MASS MEDIA

By chasing Boris Berezovsky and Vladimir Gusinsky out of the country with the specter of corruption indictments, Putin acquired control not only over their ORT, TV-6, and NTV television stations but also an impressive stable of their newspapers and radio stations. These moves, incidentally, were not unpopular, as the average citizen considered Berezovsky and Gusinsky criminals who stole the bulk of Russia's wealth upon the USSR's disintegration. Like fellow oligarch Mikhail Khodorkovsky, who would be jailed by Putin in 2003, they were also Jewish—and known to be so by Russian society—which due to widespread anti-Semitism in Russian society reinforced the popularity of Putin's moves. With the failure of TVS in June 2003, there were no more private television stations capable of reaching the length and breadth of a land that spanned eleven time zones. In 2005, the Gazprom-Media group took over the influential newspaper *Izvestiya,* which thereafter hewed closely to the government line. Then in August 2006 a steel magnate with close ties to Gazprom purchased the lively paper *Kommersant.* By 2008 some 90 percent of the Russian media was directly or indirectly in government hands.

In case after case, the same pattern emerged: the government—now awash in funds from rising world oil and natural gas prices—either infiltrated a given media organization in what was in effect a hostile financial takeover or took it to court and acquired effective control of the company. Consequently, by 2006, the Russian government, meaning Putin's Presidential Administration, controlled all five television stations capable of broadcasting to national audiences, and they accounted for more than 90 percent of all programs with political content. As a rule, these stations issued exclusively positive or neutral information about governmental activities. If problems were mentioned at all, reports focused on the effective measures that the government was allegedly taking to solve them.

To be clear, Putin did not reinstate the comprehensive control of the media that was characteristic of the Soviet era. The Internet in Putin's Russia, unlike that in China, is not censored, and a number of independent newspapers, radio stations, and even one television station remain free of formal governmental control (albeit with limited broadcast range outside Moscow). One can also buy a wide range of books, magazines, and scholarly journals containing often highly critical views of the government. Putin's government has been satisfied with its predominant control of national television news, from which some 85 percent of the Russian population derives its information about public affairs.

The government's ability to shape the public agenda was further reinforced by the general atmosphere of caution that the administrative reach of Putin's state engendered. Self-censorship instead of formal censorship has tended to be the rule. For instance, when Boris Yeltsin died in April 2007, the fearlessly independent radio station Ekho Moskvy interviewed everybody of prominence who had known and worked with (or against) Yeltsin that it could. But no one talked to Boris Berezovsky. Yeltsin's éminence grise for years, Berezovsky had fallen out of Putin's graces and was not interviewed from his exile in London even though the station's staff had Berezovsky's personal cell phone number. Ekho's editor and founder, the brave Aleksei Venediktov, was perplexed and outraged. Asked for an explanation, his staff members told Venediktov that they had indeed thought of interviewing Berezovsky but concluded that interviewing Putin's foremost enemy would attract undue attention to the station and upset the fragile understandings that the station had reached with the authorities.[22]

Putin's government used other administrative tools to shape the impact of undesired information, all the while remaining formally within the letter of the law. For instance, in late winter of 2008, two former Russian government officials, Boris Nemtsov and Vladimir Milov, issued a devastating report on the failures of Putin's government and named people in Putin's circle in connection with specific charges of corruption and mismanagement.[23] When rumors of the report's imminent publication reached the government, it reacted with alarm, especially in light of the upcoming presidential election and the anticipated transfer of presidential power from Putin to his anointed successor, Dmitri Medvedev. The government did not arrest the authors or shut down the publisher, the independent newspaper *Novaya Gazeta*. Instead, behind the scenes, the authorities strong-armed news outlets and bookstores. As a result, while Nemtsov and Milov's report was published in Russia, it could be sold only at a single kiosk in the entire country, the one in Moscow that *Novaya Gazeta* actually owned. The report fizzled and had no political impact.

Putin's Russia has become a dangerous place for the exercise of independent, critical journalism. Nearly two dozen journalists, including Paul Klebnikov, the American editor of *Forbes Russia*, have been murdered in the Putin years; all of them had been critical of the government. Authorities hardly ever investigated or prosecuted their murders seriously. In 2003 Yuri Shchekochikhin, a hardy journalist and fierce critic of the Chechen war who was investigating possible government complicity in the September 1999 apartment bombings in Moscow, died at age 53 from complete organ failure in a Russian hospital; friends and family suspect he was poisoned with the deadly agent thallium, a sign of a typical FSB rubout.[24]

In the most infamous case, reporter Anna Politkovskaya, like Shchekochikhin a fearless critic of the Russian military's conduct of the war in Chechnya, was murdered outside her apartment building in Moscow on October 7, 2006 (Putin's birthday, coincidentally). (For an example of Politkovskaya's work, see her book, *Putin's Russia* [London: Harvill Press, 2004].) She had first been shot four times, and then, in a grisly coup de grâce, a final bullet was shot into her head at point blank range. Her "body was then dumped in the lift of her apartment block."[25] Although the trail seemed to lead not to the Kremlin but to the regional and military authorities in Chechnya—where Politkovskaya had been investigating corruption and torture leads—Putin observed a meticulous silence for three days after the murder. Then, on the day of Politkovskaya's funeral, he declared that he had no reason to have her killed. After all, he maintained, her publications had had no effect on the political life of the country! Putin further insulted the dead woman by insinuating that her murder was much more damaging to the government than was her journalism, implying that it was the government, and he personally, that was the aggrieved party.[26] In so doing, Putin sent a clear signal to the Russian bureaucracy that the government would tolerate even violent suppression of dissent. Politkovskaya's employer, the newspaper *Novaya Gazeta*, which was the last major independent and critical newspaper in the country, got the message. Editors prudently began to mute the newspaper's "voice" out of concern for the safety of their staff.[27]

The control that Putin established over the dissemination of political news became an essential part of his political machine. The extent of the government's grip over the media may be gauged by Freedom House's evaluation of press freedom in Russia. In 2007, Russia was ranked 147th out of 179 countries, falling in the unfree category next to Venezuela and Chad. The report had no political resonance in Russia whatsoever, in spite of being cited in the Russian press.[28] By 2010, Russia's ranking fell to 175 out of 196 countries, behind Yemen (173rd) but ahead of Saudi Arabia (178th) and China (181st).[29]

"PUTINISM"

The practical monopoly that Putin's government exercised over televised news has greatly assisted the practice of what British scholar Andrew Wilson has termed "virtual politics."[30] Building on the psychological insight that resistance to a future eventuality tends to wane as the perception of its inevitability grows, Putin successfully created an extra-constitutional political machine that steadily reinforced the idea that he was Russia's indispensable leader.

What, then, is the essence of "Putinism"?[31] It is neither communist nor capitalist, neither totalitarian nor liberal democratic. Instead, Putin has created a distinctive, post-Soviet political amalgam that Russian political scientist Dmitri Trenin has characterized as "unconsolidated authoritarianism" (as opposed to "unconsolidated democracy") and that I term "Potemkin democracy."[32] At the heart of this system lies a political machine that is comparable to the one-party political systems characteristic at one time of certain major U.S. cities (Boss Tweed's New York, Richard Daley's Chicago); the operations of the Democratic Party under the Jim Crow laws throughout much of the American South; and long-lived national one-party systems presided over by the Liberal Democratic Party in Japan, the Revolutionary-Institutional Party in Mexico, or the Christian Democratic Party in Cold War Italy.[33]

The establishment of such machines is facilitated by the virtual exclusion of key opposition parties from competing effectively for power–think of the Communists in Italy after 1948 (excluded owing to the Cold War) or the Republicans in the American South between 1877 and 1965. In Russia, the hardships of the 1990s discredited liberal democrats while the Communists, now a reactionary party, have been unable to sufficiently expand their base beyond the older generation in order to make a credible claim to power. Under such conditions, it becomes easier for a disciplined political organization–like the machine that Putin created–to dominate political space, and the rule of a single party or organization–itself often dominated by a populist "boss"–is compatible with the legal existence of other, even opposition, political parties; a nominally free press; a substantial market economy; and even regular elections. The foundation of the ruling party's power lies in its capacity to create and exploit connections among the party, the government, and key sectors of the economy so as to make the functioning of the state, as well as critical sectors of the economy, unthinkable without the prior acquiescence of the party and its leadership. Relatedly, such a regime exploits these multiple levers of power to cultivate an air of inevitability about itself, so that the triumph of any opposition itself becomes unthinkable for most of the population.

Having won pro-government majorities in the Duma in December 1999 and his own election in March 2000, Putin moved quickly and aggressively to minimize the capacity of independent actors to constrain his freedom of action as president. In brief, Putin's Presidential Administration was able to neutralize or eliminate the practical institutional independence of every major political body and network in the country and thus reduce the chance that powerful opposition coalitions might be built. Effective government control of the mass media, hence allowing most Russians only to hear the government's point of view on sensitive issues, has powerfully reinforced the grip of Putin's machine.

In his first year as president, Putin quickly reorganized Russia's eighty-nine (later consolidated to eighty-three) federal regions into seven super regions that corresponded to Russia's military districts and appointed their supervisors, who were drawn mainly from the military and intelligence services. In additional steps to reduce these regions' power to resist the Kremlin's prerogatives, Putin removed regional governors from the Federal Assembly, the upper house of the Russian parliament, and consigned them to a symbolic presidential advisory council. Regional leaders thus no longer had an independent national forum in which to express their concerns. As part of a further centralization of presidential authority after the 2004 Beslan hostage crisis, Putin changed the rules for selecting regional governors. Henceforward, the Russian president—not the voters in the region—would appoint them. Moreover, Putin could dismiss the governors if a court could show they had violated federal law more than once. These rules made every regional leader a virtual hostage of the Kremlin. Most Russians, however, accepted these actions as necessary to clamp down on corrupt and criminalized local power cliques.

GOVERNMENTAL ADMINISTRATION

Putin staffed the Presidential Administration, government, and parliament with allies and clients drawn from circles known to be fiercely loyal to him. These groups included a St. Petersburg network going back to Putin's days as a senior official in the mayor's office there, as well as the military and the intelligence services, where Putin himself served for years as a professional intelligence officer in the KGB. Such appointees became especially prominent in the Presidential Administration, which reports directly to the Office of the President; it was composed of approximately forty thousand officials who, in effect, constitute a parallel government. The establishment of United Russia and Fair Russia as pro-Putin parties meant that Russian politics worked according to hierarchical lines of integrated government flowing from the president to the parliament via the Presidential Administration and not according to the formal constitutional provisions of the separation of powers and checks and balances. Presidential appointments to and financing of the Central Election Commission ensured that laws and rules would be interpreted to favor the Kremlin's candidates.

Putin's Presidential Administration came to control some 40 percent or more of Russia's economy. Illustratively, corporate stock owned by the government increased from 11 percent to 40 percent between 2003 and 2007.[34] (Perhaps fewer than a dozen officials, all of whom were tightly integrated into Putin's political machine, oversaw the workings of vast reaches of the economy. This group included Prime Minister Mikhail Fradkov, chairman of the board of Gazprom after Dmitri Medvedev, and Medvedev himself, formerly the head of Putin's Presidential Administration and first deputy prime minister, one-time head of Gazprom, Russia's state-controlled natural gas monopoly, and Putin's anointed successor as Russian president. By creating a series of state-supervised corporate consortia in such areas as energy, aviation, nuclear energy, arms exports, and nanotechnology, Putin aimed not only to secure greater revenues for the state but also to stimulate industrial recovery and lay the foundations for a competitive postindustrial economy in Russia. Yet such concentration of economic power in the hands of the state, given the weakness of Russia's legal system and the obscurity of political decision making, tended to reinforce systematic patterns of corruption that worked at cross-purposes with Putin's objectives.

One consequence of the global financial crisis triggered in the United States in the fall of 2008 was that the Russian government further consolidated its grip on the economy. Economic circumstances forced many of Russia's leading private firms—which were in hock to the tune of $500 billion to Western creditors, with some $130 billion in debt service due in 2009—to seek lines of credit from the government. In exchange, these corporations had to accept increased government influence over their management. Consequently, and in spite of Putin's clear determination to avoid a return to the comprehensive state ownership of the Soviet period, a creeping de facto renationalization of huge swaths of the Russian economy was taking place, further crowding out private capital and reinforcing the weight of state capitalism in Russia.

THE JUDICIAL SYSTEM

In the overwhelming majority of the millions of legal cases that are handled in Russia each year, the outcomes are decided on the basis of codified law as interpreted by judges and without political pressure.[35] This situation changes, however, when the political and economic interests of the Kremlin are involved. Putin has ordered a series of arrests for individuals opposed to his political preferences. They have been successfully prosecuted and given long jail sentences, sending the message that the Kremlin was not to be opposed on key political and economic issues. Most spectacularly, oil magnate Mikhail Khodorkovsky, who was both negotiating with foreign oil companies independently of the Kremlin and trying to fund political opposition to Putin, was convicted on corruption charges and sentenced to a long jail sentence.[36] The government seized his corporation, Yukos, arguably the most successful large-scale business concern in Russia, and auctioned it off at cut-rate prices to pro-Kremlin interests. Khodorkovsky's arrest signified that no large-scale business operation, especially in the field of energy, could act against the Kremlin's express wishes and in particular engage in political activity hostile to Putin.

Khodorkovsky engaged in breathtakingly cynical and illegal corporate takeover practices in the mid-1990s. Yet he was not prosecuted for these actions. The behavior of dozens of other Russian businessmen at the time (and later) could hardly be distinguished from that of Khodorkovsky, and yet they remained at large. Moreover, Khodorkovsky actually invested in his firm. By the time of his arrest, Yukos was universally conceded in Russia and abroad to be the best-run large company in the country. Rather, what put Khodorkovsky in jail was his violation of the "law of rules," not the rule of law; that is, he dared to cross Putin politically. He not only possessed the resources to make good on his challenge to Kremlin interests, but he also boasted publicly and quite imprudently of his ambition to convert his immense wealth into political power.[37] Indeed, had he succeeded in forging an alliance between Yukos and American energy firms (including ExxonMobil), Khodorkovsky would have overseen enormous revenue flows from energy receipts and pipeline tolls and emerged as a formidable political and even foreign policy actor in his own right.

In a dramatic exchange, on February 19, 2003, Putin issued a warning that Khodorkovsky ignored when he challenged Putin during a Kremlin conference on the sale of the oil firm Rosneft and implied that Putin's entourage was corrupt. "Mr. Khodorkovsky," Putin quietly queried, "are you really sure that your taxes are in order?" Khodorkovsky replied confidently, "Absolutely." "Well," said Putin, "that's what we are going to find out."[38]

In the end, Khodorkovsky was arrested, pronounced guilty, and sentenced to a long term in a Siberian prison colony. The patently political nature of the case is illustrated by the fact that the court's sentence was copied from the prosecutor's indictment, even including its grammatical and typographical errors.[39] Prosecutor, judge, and jury were one and the same, as was always true of political cases in Soviet Russia.

As of this writing, Khodorkovsky still sits in a Siberian jail. The government issued new indictments against him in March 2009 and engineered a fourteen-year term (including time served) on patently spurious embezzlement and money laundering charges. Eleven days before the court passed judgment on December 27, 2010, Putin publicly stated in reference to the case, "A thief belongs behind bars."[40] The Khodorkovsky case shows how the judicial system has been subordinated to the Kremlin's interests, thereby deterring business challenges to the regime. His case also sent a signal to investors about the legal security of their holdings, with disturbing long-term implications for direct private investment in the economic development of Russia. State control over physical assets thereby became more important than the rule of law. In 2007, Freedom House ranked the Russian judicial system 170th out of 199 countries in terms of its independence from political authority, thereby again placing Russia among the most unfree nations of the world. President Medvedev himself stated in September 2009, "[Human rights abuses] are so numerous because there is no effective judiciary system."[41]

PUTIN CHECKMATES CHESS CHAMPION KASPAROV

A striking example of the Putin machine's abusive extralegal persecutions involves the Russian government's successful effort to undermine former world chess champion Garry Kasparov's quixotic run for the Russian presidency between 2005 and 2007. One of the most famous names in chess-mad Russia, Kasparov abandoned his chess career in March 2005 after the Beslan school massacre, charging the government with incompetence and even complicity in the catastrophe. Kasparov accused Putin of running a "criminal" regime and of manipulating tensions in the Caucasus for his electoral benefit. Considered even by friends to suffer from egomaniacal tendencies, Kasparov bravely confronted Putin whenever he could, calling for the replacement of Putin's regime by a liberal government along Western lines.

It is doubtful that Kasparov–calling for the Westernization of Russia–could ever have achieved much electoral success in a country that was still recovering from the disastrous economic and social consequences of the 1990s, when Western influence in Russia had been at its peak. Still, Putin and his lieutenants took no chances. Wherever Kasparov went to speak out against Putin, his path was blocked, at times literally. For instance, when flying into the Caucasus, Kasparov often found that the airport's runway was littered with boulders or cows. Once, in Stavropol, his hosts arrived at the airport too late; the traffic police had held them up until the crowd waiting for Kasparov went home. Auditoriums that had been booked for his speeches regularly experienced sudden power outages just before his arrival. In other cases, local authorities declared building code violations that required the public to be evacuated. In one public library in Rostov-on-the-Don, a water pipe broke, and Kasparov's planned talk was canceled. Everywhere that Kasparov went, he was followed by the FSB secret police, who openly tailed him. As for Kasparov and his entourage, they often found that all of the hotels in a city were booked, but no one else seemed to have problems finding rooms.

The state-controlled media either ignored Kasparov or presented truncated versions of his talks and interviews so that it seemed that he was only talking about chess. Further, the media rigorously observed a tacit ban on live interviews with him. The regime's message that Kasparov was persona non grata was thus successfully transmitted. Even one restaurant's head waiter, alarmed that Kasparov had entered for dinner, exclaimed, "In God's name get out, or I'll be in big trouble!"[42]

In the end, a frustrated and exhausted Kasparov–who had been arrested and briefly detained during a political rally in Moscow in April 2007–abandoned his quest for the Russian presidency. Putin's machine had checkmated the greatest chess master in the world.

POLITICAL SYMBOLISM

In addition to measures of selective and subtle repression, Putin took care to associate his policies with a series of highly visible and emotional symbols that responded to broadly felt Russian psychological needs. He invoked tradition, after the radical break with the past constituted by the Soviet collapse; he stressed order and social security, after the economic, social, and institutional collapse of the 1990s; and he sought international respect, after the collapse of the Soviet alliance system and the advance of NATO in the 1990s. He reintroduced the old Soviet national anthem (though without the pro-Stalin lyrics), a stirring piece first adopted during the Second World War and associated by many Russians with state grandeur. He adopted the czarist era's symbol of the double-headed eagle with three crowns as Russia's state emblem. He also sponsored highly visible foreign policy acts such as announcing Russia's withdrawal from the Conventional Forces in Europe Treaty in the summer of 2007. Most moving for Russia's Christian majority, Putin successfully encouraged the unification of the domestic and foreign branches of the Russian Orthodox Church, which had been sent asunder by the Russian Revolution.

Putin carefully employed political symbolism to reinforce mass sentiment while avoiding painful fault lines in Russian society. He opposed removing Lenin's body from display in the mausoleum in Red Square, believing that it would be a needless and harmful provocation to scores of millions of Russians who had been socialized under Lenin's auspices. At a Kremlin press conference on July 18, 2001, he explained,

> The country lived under the monopoly of power of the Soviet Communist Party for 70 years. This period amounts to an entire lifetime and many people connect their lives with Lenin's name. For them the burial of Lenin would mean that they lived according to sham values, followed a false path and that their lives had been lived in vain.

Given that a certain political consensus had finally been achieved in Russian society, burying Lenin, according to Putin, could destroy that consensus and "hinder the practical modernization of Russia." If Russia could successfully modernize, society's values would change accordingly, and such questions would eventually resolve themselves under changed future conditions.[43]

Similarly, while Putin has spoken favorably of Stalin as an architect both of the Russians' victory over the Nazis and of Soviet Russia's superpower status, Putin on several occasions has spoken movingly about the victims of Stalin's terror as part of the tragic fabric of Russia's twentieth-century history. And while Putin's Education Ministry has sponsored history texts that tend to white-wash the dimensions of Stalin's crimes, Russian high school students are now required to read passages from *Gulag Archipelago*, Aleksandr Solzhentsyn's devastating indictment of Stalin's concentration camp system.

In these ways, Putin cultivated a charismatic aspect of his political power, one that sought to portray him as the leader of all the people. In the process, Putin mobilized a degree of mass support that has proved remarkably resilient and independent of the deep contempt with which most Russians hold the actual performance of the Russian government and bureaucracy. While the "government" generally earns approval ratings of less than 20 percent, Putin's approval ratings ranged from 68 to 87 percent throughout most of his presidency.[44]

BOUNDARIES OF POWER

For all the impressive aura of authority surrounding his presidency, Putin was no dictator. Nor was his affinity for authoritarian rule similar to the unbridled totalitarianism of Soviet days. Substantial sectors of the economy remained in private hands, including scores of billions of dollars in liquid capital in private bank accounts abroad. A considerable public forum existed for debate on public issues, though much more so in the press than on television. Furthermore, Russians had the right to travel abroad pretty much as they pleased; availability of funds, not political considerations, was their main constraint. Religious adherents of Russia's historical religions of Orthodox Christianity, Islam, Judaism, and Buddhism were free to practice their faith more or less as they pleased. Putin's Russia, measured by any Cold War standard, represented impressive progress from the Soviet period.

Meanwhile, Putin has not been able to implement all that he wanted. In a major policy failure, in January 2005 he attempted a wide-ranging social security reform by replacing government-provided social benefits and services (free or low-cost public transportation for seniors and veterans, subsidized rents, etc.) with cash payments directly from the government. It quickly became apparent that the governmental bureaucracy was simply incapable of implementing such a broad, nationwide reform. In the face of growing public protest, above all from the elderly, the government backed down and abandoned the project.

More broadly, Putin's concentration of power in the Russian state failed to address deep-seated flaws in Russia's economy and society. He allowed the economy to remain far too dependent on petroleum and raw materials exports. Putin failed to establish a true civil service or to control the crime rate. (Russia suffers from a murder rate four to five times that of the United States, otherwise by far the highest in the industrialized world.) The rate of HIV infection continues to grow, and life expectancy for Russian males remains low (less than sixty one years of age). Draft evasion is high, and the physical and mental debility of those inducted (at least one-third) constitutes a major limitation on the country's military potential.[45]

Most damaging to Putin's capacity to govern effectively, corruption flourished. As discussed earlier, in a stunning 2008 report that alarmed Putin's government, ex–government officials Boris Nemtsov and Vladimir Milov sketched the breadth and depth of governmental corruption under Putin. They claimed that political corruption in Russia grew nearly tenfold between 1999 and 2008, fueled by the combination of enormous energy receipts and an increasingly authoritarian state–capitalist regime. Many government officials, on an average salary of some $700–800 per month, actually take home close to $1 million per year. Russians in the know report a very specific price list for various services in the upper reaches of the Russian bureaucracy. They claim the costs for obtaining various appointments are as follows:

- an ordinary police official, $50,000 to $100,000;
- a senior police official in Moscow, $500,000;
- a judgeship, up to $300,000;
- a senior official in customs, more than $1 million;
- a senator in the Federation Council, up to $6 million; and
- a senior government minister, up to $10 million.[46]

Not surprisingly, the European Police Office (Europol) has declared that 20 percent of Russian members of the Duma, 40 percent of decision makers in private business, 50 percent of bank directors, and 60 percent of directors and managers of state-owned businesses are tied to the criminal world.[47]

Nemtsov and Milov's assertions went even further. Calculating the annual "corruption tax" at more than $300 billion (or roughly 20 percent of Russian GDP), the authors took direct aim at the foundation of Putin's machine, namely, the government-controlled natural gas monopoly Gazprom. They identified a network involving close Putin associates as the fulcrum of an enormous swindle at the Russian government's epicenter.[48] In July 2005 a circle of Putin's associates had managed to purchase Gazprom-Media for less than 3 percent of its actual value, giving it control of all but one of Russia's national television stations.[49]

In a stunning example of piracy that Putin claimed to have eradicated, in September 2005, Putin friend and financial baron Roman Abramovich sold 75 percent of the stock of the oil firm Sibneft for $13.7 billion, half of which was financed by Putin's government and half by Gazprom. Abramovich had paid just $100 million for the firm back in the 1990s. In effect, the Russian government paid Abramovich $7 billion to expand government stock in Gazprom, a firm that the government already controlled.[50]

As previously noted, in 2010 Transparency International rated Russia one of the most corrupt societies on earth at 154th among 178 countries studied. Likewise, the World Bank in 2010 ranked Russia as one of the most difficult countries in the world in which to do business, at 123 out of 183 countries evaluated, just behind Uganda. In the critical area of dealing with construction permits, Russia ranked next to last, at 182 out of 183.[51] So pervasive was the problem that in June 2009 the Swedish furniture maker Ikea—declaring a policy of zero tolerance for corruption—decided to suspend its substantial investment in Russia. Clearly, the country's economic future is at risk if governmental corruption is not brought under some degree of control.[52] Yet Putin's model of governance, by reinforcing the nexus of business and politics, seemed to make the problem worse. Greater transparency in decision making and genuine competition among economic and political actors were clearly required to reduce corruption's grip on the land, but there was little sign, after a decade in power, that Putin's system had an answer to this problem.

FROM PRESIDENT PUTIN TO PRESIDENT MEDVEDEV

Throughout the summer and fall of 2007, the greatest fear of the Russian political elite and, judging by opinion polls, much of Russian society was that Vladimir Putin might actually observe the terms of the Russian Constitution and step down as president after two terms in office.[53] Many felt that there were few, if any, candidates who could ensure the stability that Putin had undoubtedly provided, especially by contrast with the Yeltsin years. More specifically, the Russian political class understood that Putin had maintained a precarious balance of power among influential political and economic factions. What bound these factions together was the confidence that under Putin the privatization of the Russian economy that took place in the 1990s would not be reversed, so long as fealty to the Russian leader was displayed.[54]

As the March 2, 2008, election drew near, Putin shrewdly kept his intentions private. Seeking to avoid the lame-duck mantle and to maintain control over the electoral process, Putin deferred the naming of an heir apparent as long as possible. All the while he gave an equal nod to two longtime protégés from St. Petersburg, Sergei Ivanov and Dmitri Medvedev, who were then serving as first deputy prime ministers with responsibilities for the military-industrial economy and social welfare, respectively. Putin made it clear, and nobody with clout challenged him, that he alone would choose his successor and that he would continue to wield political influence even after he stepped down as president. As he told the Russian public in October 2006,

> Even after I no longer have my presidential powers . . . I will be able to hold on to what is most important and valuable to any politician: your trust. And, using this, we will be able to influence life in our country, to guarantee that it develops in a continuous manner so as to have an impact on what happens in Russia.[55]

In October 2007, Putin announced that he would stand as the head of the United Russia Party in the parliamentary elections to be held in December, positioning himself to become prime minister after stepping down as president. In effect, a vote for United Russia was a vote for Putin, turning the parliamentary election into a referendum on Putin's presidency and on Putin himself. In an election that West European monitors declared unfair, United Russia won 64 percent of the votes and 70 percent of the seats in parliament, thereby acquiring a supermajority that would allow Putin as prime minister to pass constitutional amendments and even, in principle, to impeach the president. In this way, Putin could maintain effective control over the Russian political system even while occupying the nominally inferior post of prime minister.

Whoever succeeded Putin would have to come to terms with the following facts:

- Putin was head of United Russia, which controlled 70 percent of parliamentary seats directly.
- United Russia itself was made up of Putin appointees and loyalists.
- Putin's party could move a bill of impeachment against the president with near impunity.
- Putin retained the intense loyalty of the armed forces and paramilitary services because of his conduct of the war in Chechnya and his stand against terrorism.
- Putin retained charismatic legitimacy among the electorate that was independent of his formal position in the government.
- Putin undoubtedly had control of key personnel files, compiled by the intelligence services, that could be deployed at a moment's notice against anyone seeking to challenge his authority.

In a powerful display of his unquestioned power, a week after the parliamentary elections Putin announced that he would support Dmitri Medvedev as his heir apparent. The very next day, Medvedev offered to appoint Putin as his prime minister, an offer that Putin publicly accepted a week later. The ensuing presidential election campaign was virtually a Putin pageant. Medvedev made only one campaign appearance, making it clear that he hoped to be elected on Putin's coattails. He would be bound, he said, "to continue the course that has proven its effectiveness over the last eight years, the course of President Putin."[56] All televised campaign spots made the same point: a vote for Medvedev was a vote for Putin.[57]

Medvedev won the presidency with 71 percent of the vote. Executive power in Russia had been transferred primarily as a result of court politics, the elections themselves having been reduced to formalities for the ratification of presidential preference. Indeed, Russia remained the only country in postcommunist Europe where power had yet to change hands through genuinely free and fair elections.

This situation did not seem to trouble a majority of Russians, who were experiencing the tenth consecutive year of economic growth and improving living standards. As the harsh Putin critic Yevgeniya Albats put it, Putin was

A newly wedded couple kisses in front of an election poster showing Putin and presidential candidate Dmitri Medvedev in Moscow (March 1, 2008). Shen Bohan/Xinhua Press/Corbis

an accurate reflection of the mood of Russian society, projecting the hopes and fears of countless Russians desperate for order and stability after the chaos of the previous decade.[58] In effect, most Russians were not demanding liberal democracy, and Putin was not supplying it.[59]

6

PUTIN IN POWER: FOREIGN POLICY

"We have been weak and the weak are beaten."
— *Vladimir Putin, 2004*[1]

Throughout Putin's eight years as president, the main focus of his foreign policy was to engineer a partnership with the United States and Western Europe while at the same time consolidating Russian predominance among the post-Soviet countries of central Eurasia. While often frustrated by the West's resistance to his notion of partnership, Putin never entertained illusions that alliances elsewhere, for instance with China, could compensate for the centrality of Russia's dense and complex set of relationships with Western Europe, North America, and Japan (the Group of Seven, or G-7). Time and again, most dramatically at the Davos world economic summit in January 2009, Putin (now as prime minister) made it clear that Russia had no alternative to working out its relationships with the G-7 world.[2]

Putin himself has dominated the making of Russian foreign policy. Whatever the formal institutions of Russia's national security and diplomatic decision-making machinery, Putin's word has been decisive on all issues that interest him. Time and again, he has undertaken dramatic moves, never hesitating to go against deeply entrenched institutional interests. Acting boldly in September 2001, he decided to ally with the United States against al Qaeda and the Taliban in Afghanistan. In this case, Putin flouted the broadly held view among Russia's national security elites that the United States should be left to stew in its own juices there. When eighteen retired generals issued a public protest against Putin's acquiescence to the U.S. military establishing bases in post-Soviet Central Asia, he prevailed easily. Since then, Putin has continued to control foreign and national security policy, as shown when he cut off natural gas supplies to Ukraine in the winters of 2006 and 2009 and with his direction of Russia's war with Georgia in August 2008.

In practice, Putin's foreign policy moved Russia in a nationalist direction. As Russia became stronger, he became less interested in integrating it into Western international structures. His dramatic decision (later reversed) in June 2009 to withdraw Russia's application for membership in the World Trade Organization, which embodies Western economic and legal principles, underscored this point. Nor was he inclined any longer to listen to what either the European Union or the United States had to say about the Russian government's persistent violation of international legal and human rights norms.

But Putin did not seek to challenge Western capitalist structures and international institutions in the old Soviet ideological manner. He preferred to conduct relations with the transatlantic community on the basis of Realpolitik, in which pragmatic self-interest prevailed. At the same time, Putin wanted to consolidate Russia's position as the center of its own geopolitical universe. That universe centered on the lands of the former Soviet Union in central Eurasia, where he repeatedly deployed Russia's considerable array of assets—above all, the energy card—to underwrite a *Monrovskaya Doktrina,* or a Russian-style "Monroe Doctrine."

PUTIN'S FOREIGN POLICY INHERITANCE

By the time Vladimir Putin assumed supreme power in Russia in early 2000, the country had already been through a wrenching series of convulsions at home and abroad. Russia's initial enthusiasm for integration into Western economic, political, and security institutions had been squelched by NATO's expansion, which was punctuated by NATO's air war against Russia's ally Serbia in the spring of 1999. By the end of the 1990s, hardly any Russian domestic reformer advocated a foreign policy of liberal internationalism.

The generally positive view that many ordinary Russians had of the United States historically—based on memories of a shared alliance against Adolf Hitler and frankly idealized images of the American way of life—came to an end with the resolution of the Cold War and the disappointments of the 1990s. America's intimate involvement in the economic initiatives of the Yeltsin years meant that most Russians now identified Washington with the economic misery and social collapse that defined that decade-long "time of troubles" after the Cold War ended. To most Russians, including Russia's dwindling band of liberal democrats, the United States seemed bent on maximizing its power advantage over Russia at a time when Russia was too weak to resist. The cold logic of power rather than communities of shared values and interests appeared to govern U.S. relations with Russia. Russians, in fact, reached this conclusion not during the "unilateralist" presidency of George W. Bush (2001–2009) but during the Clinton years (1993–2001). They believed that Washington was trying to dictate policy, and they came to see the misery and chaos of the 1990s not as the betrayal of liberal democracy but as its very essence.[3]

Russia in the 1990s went through a foreign policy evolution comparable in many respects to that experienced by Soviet Russia's communist rulers in their first years in power between 1917 and 1925. In each case, a government had been established in a seemingly radical departure from the past. The Bolsheviks repudiated the international policy as well as the domestic practices of both imperial Russia and the fledgling democratic government that briefly followed it in the expectation of an imminent global communist revolution that they believed would finally integrate Russia with the economically most advanced countries of the world. Likewise, Russia's democratic rulers in the early 1990s, in repudiating communism and formal empire, expected that Russia would join the community of wealthy democratic states as a peer and in this way would also achieve the integration of Russia with the most advanced states in the world. In each case, Russia's rulers rejected classical interest-based foreign policies in favor of an ideologically based diplomacy, one that defined Russia's interests as a byproduct of the government's political aspirations. Boris Yeltsin hoped that his democratic and capitalist ambitions would ease the path for the country's entrance into a global community of prosperous democracies where communities of liberal values would render balances of power irrelevant.

The post-Soviet transit toward a more sober, state interest–based approach was symbolized by the replacement of the liberal democrat Andrei Kozyrev as foreign minister in early 1996 with the venerable statist Yevgeny Primakov. Gone was the idea that Russia would somehow be absorbed into the Western international political economy managed by the United States. While Primakov strove to bring about a multipolar world to check the seemingly unbridled power of the United States in world affairs, he had no illusions about the difficulty of this task or the hopelessness of a frontal challenge to the U.S.-centric international order. Subsequently, Putin often expressed his respect for Prima-kov's contribution to the evolution of Russian foreign policy in the post–Cold War era and maintained a cordial relationship with him.

In sum, Russia's evident lack of payoff for exercising its liberal option in foreign affairs and at home helped to spur the rise of a more nationalist frame for the conduct of foreign policy. Again, this development happened well be-fore Vladimir Putin assumed the reins of supreme political power in Russia as prime minister in August 1999 and president in March 2000. The notion that it was Putin who buried Russia's liberal alternatives at home and abroad is dis-proved by the course of events during the Yeltsin years (1992–1999).

PUTIN'S FOREIGN POLICY BEFORE 9/11

Putin is best understood as a pragmatic, modern realist who thinks in terms of raw power–economic, military, and political. He sees the world as intensely and fundamentally competitive. In many ways, his foreign policy outlook re-sembles that of the American "power realists," or Republican conservatives. His worldview is completely devoid of abstract ideological categories, and he is painfully conscious of the limitations of Russian power in a post-Soviet, post–Cold War world.

When Putin became president of Russia, he hoped his country would be recognized as one of the great powers of the world, but he also understood that he had been dealt a weak economic hand and that Moscow would have to pursue an especially skillful and prudent diplomacy.[4] Putin's Russia could not afford expansive international ambitions. Rather, Russia's primary foreign policy tasks were to maximize relationships that were economically profitable and to minimize external challenges to the country's natural sphere of influ-ence along its post-Soviet borderlands. Putin grasped that Russia could not afford enemies. As far as Russia's immediate neighborhood was concerned, he wanted to establish Russia as the center of its own regional system of states, relying on its overwhelming power in the region and its control of those energy resources that its neighbors needed. The overarching challenge for Russian diplomacy under Putin was to ensure that these two vital trajectories of Rus-sian interests–good relations with the West and dominance in the post-Soviet region–did not work at cross-purposes with each other.

Putin immediately adopted a pragmatic approach, reflecting a reasoned acquiescence in what Moscow could neither control nor oppose. He abandoned histrionic opposition to NATO expansion toward Russia's borderlands. He even acknowledged the right of the three Baltic states, which had for half a century been part of the Soviet Union, to join the North Atlantic alliance. He also lowered the volume on Russian opposition to growing U.S. investment in strategic antiballistic missile systems.[5] Finally, in January 2001, Putin came out firmly against those in his administration who had been launching trial balloons about repudiating Russia's external sovereign debt, or the part owed to foreign governments. In a dramatic display of his emerging presidential authority, he made clear that he would have no part in reestablishing the country's isolation from the world economy, an isolation that he identified as a major failing of the Soviet system.

From the outset, then, Putin underscored that Russian foreign policy should be pragmatic and promote the country's internal political and economic development. In a major early address to the Russian Federal Assembly, he emphasized,

> It is important to have a solid reputation in politics as well as in economics; therefore, we should strictly carry out our long-term [international] obligations and agreements and so uphold those principles according to which we are developing our relations with other states. . . .
>
> I wish to emphasize that . . . the prosperity of our country and its citizens, the fate of our countrymen abroad and not least of all success in our own internal affairs depend on how intelligently, subtly and effectively we implement our foreign policy.[6]

For all of Putin's appeals to a subtle and pragmatic realism in foreign policy, it was a predominantly reactive approach to Russia's external challenges. In the months before the terror attacks on U.S. soil on September 11, 2001, Putin's Russia, as with so much of the rest of the world, was anxiously absorbing signs that the Bush administration was seeking to repudiate multilateralism and cement a permanent American hegemony in world affairs. And while President Bush may have claimed to see "into Putin's soul" during their June 2001 summit meeting in Slovenia, no one could have foretold the dramatic reversal of roles that would take place after the 9/11 attacks.

CHECHNYA IN PUTIN'S FOREIGN POLICY CALCULATIONS

By the time of Putin's accession to power, the one area where Russia's international relationships impinged most directly and urgently on the country's domestic affairs involved the war in Chechnya. Putin's government had to isolate the Chechen rebellion from every possible source of international support, moral as well as material. Indeed, following the four terrorist bombings in Moscow in September 1999, Putin had argued forcefully, but without resonance in the West, that the second Russian-Chechen war was at heart a Russian war against international terrorism. No Western country, including the United States, denied Russia's right to defend its territorial integrity or disputed that Russia was justified in responding forcefully to the Chechens' 1999 invasion of Russian Dagestan. Unlike the Yeltsin government's experience in the first Chechen war of 1994–1996, however, Putin's government was subjected to a steady stream of criticism from Western governments and nongovernmental organizations (NGOs) about its conduct in Chechnya.

This state of affairs was ironic since Yeltsin's government had far less justification and provocation in launching the first war than Putin did in waging the second. An exhausted and distracted Clinton administration in the fall of 1999 and into 2000 voiced its concerns about the legality of the Russian military's conduct in Chechnya, if not of the war itself. At the November 1999 meeting of the Organization for Security and Cooperation in Europe (OSCE) in Istanbul, Clinton denied that the war in Chechnya was a purely internal Russian affair. American finance officials admitted that the termination of credits from the International Monetary Fund and the postponement of credits from the Export-Import Bank were related to Russia's conduct of the Chechnya war. And early in the George W. Bush administration, the State Department truly alarmed the Russian government by sponsoring a meeting between the Chechen foreign minister in exile and the department's senior specialist on Russian affairs.[7] While none of the statements or actions amounted to the U.S. government's adoption of the Chechen cause, they did underscore to Moscow that its line on the war in Chechnya could not be taken for granted in international circles. Due diligence would have to be paid in order to ensure that the Chechen rebels remained isolated from outside support.

In Western Europe, too, Russia faced opposition to its policy in Chechnya, though less from sitting governments and more from NGOs and European

*Clinton and Putin signing the Strategic Stability Cooperation Initiative
at the United Nations Millennium Summit, New York City (September 6, 2000).*
Ron Sachs/CNP/Sygma/Corbis

international organizations. Indeed, the Parliamentary Assembly of the Council of Europe in Strasbourg stripped Russia of its voting rights in April 2000 because of the Russian military's demonstrable abuses in Chechnya and the manifest unwillingness of the Russian government to investigate them.[8] Generally, though, European governments were reluctant to link Russian human rights violations in Chechnya or elsewhere to their bilateral relations or their ties between Russia and the European Union.

Western European economic interests, above all their dependence on Russian natural gas, dampened the governments' inclination to confront Russia. For instance, at the November 1999 OSCE meeting, Putin worked successfully with Western European leaders to distance themselves from Clinton's efforts to portray the Russian-Chechen war as a matter for international adjudication instead of a purely Russian internal affair. The conference's final communiqué reflected a much more qualified assessment of Russian conduct in Chechnya from that initially proposed by the United States.[9] Still, while European governments generally followed a course aimed at cooperation with, rather than isolation of, Russia, European elites now increasingly criticized human rights violations in Russia in general and in Chechnya in particular. A clash of values was emerging.

Such criticism tended to elicit harsh and often crude retorts from Putin. He was absolutely convinced of the rectitude of his cause and believed (correctly) that he had the overwhelming majority of Russians on his side. He rejected even the slightest criticism, explicit or implicit, of his policy in Chechnya. At a public international conference, Putin told a French journalist who questioned Russian policy in Chechnya that he should go to Moscow, where Putin would arrange a circumcision so that he could feel at one with his putative Muslim soul mates.[10]

In spite of such occasional outbursts, Putin proved capable of the most wide-ranging flexibility. When he learned of the terror attacks upon the United States, he took a series of astounding measures that, among other things, took the issue of Chechnya off the international agenda.

PUTIN'S FOREIGN POLICY AFTER SEPTEMBER 11, 2001

The 2001 terror attacks on the United States prompted Putin to switch deftly from a reactive to a proactive foreign policy. He was the first foreign leader to contact President Bush, and he immediately pledged unconditional support in the fight against al Qaeda and the Taliban government in Afghanistan. In a bold decision, taken against the advice of the overwhelming majority of the Russian national security establishment, Putin made Russia the most important U.S. ally in the war against the Taliban. Among other things, he accelerated deliveries of weapons to the Northern Alliance in Afghanistan so that when the Alliance marched into Kabul it did so with Russian, not American, weapons and vehicles. He encouraged the governments of Uzbekistan and Tajikistan to allow American military bases on their territory. He opened Russian airspace for American overflights to bases in Central Asia so that the United States could conduct search and rescue operations for U.S. airmen in Afghanistan. Finally, he ordered Russian intelligence agencies to cooperate completely with their American counterparts on all matters connected to al Qaeda and the Taliban.

Putin obtained two direct benefits from this newly forged Russian-American alliance. First, the United States helped Russia solve an irksome problem that Moscow could not deal with on its own: they stopped the Taliban from exporting radical Islamist fundamentalism to post-Soviet Central Asia and potentially to Russia itself, where nearly 20 percent of the population was Muslim. Washington also ceased complaining about the Russians' behavior in Chechnya. In fact, George W. Bush now fully embraced Putin's long-standing argument that the Russian war in Chechnya was part of a more general struggle against radical Islamist terror around the world.

By making Russia an indispensable ally of the United States, Putin hoped to forge a partnership with Washington, one in which each would value its overall ties and not allow any single issue to divide them.[11] Putin dropped earlier Russian rhetoric about moving toward a multipolar world. One hundred leading foreign policy figures, including former prime minister Primakov, issued a statement renouncing "multipolarity games" as "too expensive and unpragmatic." As awkward as it might have been for Russia to join a U.S.-led coalition against radical Islamic terror, it was now unthinkable to oppose the United States.[12]

Putin believed that joining the American coalition would allow Russia to gain a "voice at the table," one that the Americans would have to take into account. But once the high-intensity phase of the Afghan campaign was over

Putin and Bush in Crawford, Texas, just after the overthrow of the Taliban in Afghanistan (November 15, 2001). Bob E. Daemmrich/Sygma/Corbis

in November 2001, the United States discounted Putin's goodwill and alienated him. In December 2001, for example, just a month after Russian-armed Northern Alliance troops captured Kabul, the United States repudiated the 1972 Antiballistic Missile (ABM) Treaty, which the Russians viewed as the cornerstone of their own nuclear security. In March 2002, a report leaked from the Pentagon revealed that Russia had been added to the list of nuclear target states, in addition to such rogue states as North Korea, Iraq, and Iran. Two months later, the United States agreed to a statement on future reductions in offensive nuclear arms but without making any commitment to destroying the weapons that would be dismantled. Of course, the Russians feared that the United States might one day break out of these treaty limitations, as it recently did with the ABM Treaty.

Even more upsetting to Putin was his growing realization that Russia would not be able to exert any real influence on NATO's war planning. Nor would Russia be able to influence NATO's plans to enlarge its membership, even with respect to the former Soviet republics of Estonia, Latvia, Lithuania, Ukraine, and Georgia. The Bush administration stated publicly that the road to membership for Ukraine and Georgia remained open, and on May 9, 2002, U.S. permanent representative to NATO Nicholas Burns declared that the Caucasus and Central Asia were now areas of official interest to NATO. More offensive still, the U.S. government announced that it was determined to go to war in Iraq to effect regime change in Baghdad even if the UN Security Council, where the Russians retained a veto as one of the council's five permanent members, did not sanction the action.

These actions discredited any remaining sympathy for the United States in Russia. Even longtime pro-American liberals, such as economist Grigory Yavlinsky and historian Yuri Afanasyev, decried Washington's ingratitude. It was clearly an illusion, Afanasyev said, to think that Russia could forge a genuine partnership with the United States.[13]

Although U.S. leaders were unmoved by such Russian sentiment, Putin made one last attempt to establish a foundation of cooperation in Russian-American relations. He agreed that several hundred American troops could come to Georgia and train the Georgian military to police the porous and dangerous frontier between eastern Georgia and Russian Chechnya, where Russia was still at war with the remnants of a brutal secessionist rebellion.[14] By all accounts such cooperation went reasonably well until the pragmatic Georgian leader Eduard Shevardnadze was replaced by the anti-Russian Mikheil Saa-kashvili in January 2004. Saakashvili not only snubbed Putin's personal invita-tion to attend the ceremonies in Moscow marking the sixtieth anniversary of the Soviet victory over Nazi Germany, scheduled for May 9, 2005, but he then ostentatiously received U.S. president Bush in the Georgian capital of Tbilisi just before the Russian celebrations.[15] What happened then represents a key in-stance in how the Russian-American security relationship collapsed after 2001.

Saakashvili and Bush quickly dashed any lingering hopes of a lasting Russian-American partnership. First, Saakashvili sent two thousand Georgian troops to Iraq, calculating that they would be the ticket to the fast track to his country's admission to NATO. The Pentagon reciprocated, offering a mas-sive armament and training program for America's new military ally. Further, by keeping alive the prospect of Georgia's admission to NATO, officials in Washington encouraged Saakashvili to believe that he could escape his geog-raphy and substitute the United States for Russia in Georgia's foreign relations. Saakashvili's contempt for Moscow's regional security sensibilities triggered crippling Russian trade sanctions against Georgian fruit, vegetable, and wine exports to Russia, by far Georgia's largest market for its economically vital agricultural products. But, more important, Saakashvili's actions and Bush's reactions revealed that the United States was not interested in the kind of co-operative security arrangement that Putin had envisioned in the aftermath of 9/11. Instead, Bush administration officials believed that they were still locked in a zero-sum contest with Russia. Indeed, U.S. vice president Dick Cheney told the retired Soviet leader Mikhail Gorbachev that unflinching U.S. pressure had caused Moscow to concede in the Cold War and that there was no reason to abandon that approach in the post-Soviet period.[16]

Putin's challenge now was to advance his country's legitimate interests in a world dominated by American power and influence. Could he shape a foreign policy that would avoid the twin dangers of confrontation with the United States and isolation from the international political economy?[17]

RUSSIA AND WESTERN EUROPE

Putin believed that Russia was not simply European but *Western* European in its cultural orientation. He hoped to forge a network of economic, political, and even security ties between Russia and Europe. Within two weeks of the 9/11 attacks on the United States, he gave one of his most important foreign policy speeches to the German Bundestag in Berlin. As the first Russian head of state ever to address the German parliament, Putin made his introductory remarks in Russian, and then switched to German for the rest of the speech. Skillfully summarizing the great cultural debt that Russia owed Germany and laying particular emphasis on the legacies of Friedrich Schiller, Gotthold Lessing, Wilhelm von Humboldt, Immanuel Kant, and Johann Wolfgang Goethe in Russian arts and sciences, Putin argued for a comprehensive reassessment of the Russian-Western relationship and called for a true partnership in a post–September 11 world. He decried the isolation from world developments that had been a consequence of Soviet ideology and criticized all remnants of Cold War thinking that divided the world into two camps. Accepting the legitimacy of the American-European security relationship via NATO, he denied that NATO was a threat to Russia and implied that Russia itself might one day apply for membership.[18] Dramatically outlining his vision of Russia's international relations in the aftermath of September 11, Putin depicted a world in which Russia, Europe, and the United States faced common threats from radical Islamic terror and appealed for collaborative security measures in defense of civilizational and cultural values that Europeans, Americans, and Russians held in common.

The impact of Putin's speech in Germany can hardly be exaggerated. The German legislators' applause interrupted him fifteen times. But his hopes were soon crushed when the United States, with whom the majority of European states remained linked through NATO, spurned Putin's pleas for security collaboration. Putin realized that he would have to pursue Russian national interests chiefly on his own—without any assistance from Western Europe—while avoiding the equally unacceptable traps of isolation or confrontation.

Putin's cultural and diplomatic focus on Western Europe was based on a substantial economic foundation. Trade, finance, and investment flows were drawing post-Soviet Russia into ever-tighter webs of interdependence with the countries of the European Union. In the early Putin years, the bulk of Russia's foreign sovereign debt was owed to European and above all German creditors. Shortly after the Soviet collapse, the value of Russia's trade with both formerly communist Eastern Europe and the former Soviet republics was eclipsed by that with the Western European countries of the European Union. By 2005 the European Union had become Russia's largest trading partner, accounting for 45 percent of Russian imports and 56 percent of its export trade, the latter made up chiefly of oil and natural gas deliveries. The majority of Russia's foreign investment came from firms based in the European Union.[19] Moreover, by paying full market price for Russia's energy exports (the domestic price was heavily subsidized), the European Union was in effect subsidizing one-fourth or more of the Russian government's federal budget. Putin understood that Russian political stability as well as economic prosperity depended on sound relations with the countries of the European Union. At the same time, Europe's growing dependence on Russian natural gas deliveries—ranging from 45 percent of Germany's domestic consumption to nearly 100 percent in the Baltic states, Finland, and Bulgaria—seemed to impel the Europeans toward the kind of partnership that Putin outlined in his Bundestag speech.

WAR IN IRAQ AND THE PARIS-BERLIN-MOSCOW TROIKA

In this context, Putin made one more attempt to forge a broad Western-oriented partnership after the frustration of his efforts to build an American-Russian security community. The impetus was the U.S. government's decision to go to war to effect regime change in Iraq and the opposition that it aroused in France and Germany.[20] Putin's endeavor, too, would ultimately prove disappointing, as he would discover that Russia's short-term tactical alliances with America's NATO allies were no substitute for the deeper ties that bound them to their transatlantic protector.

Putin's government had significant bilateral interests at stake in Saddam Hussein's Iraq. These matters included a massive debt to the Soviet Union that Iraq had incurred during the Cold War and now owed to Russia as the Soviet Union's chief successor state, as well as a $40 billion trade agreement. The two items were interrelated, as the Iraqi side had promised an accelerated payment of its debt to Moscow in exchange for the trade deal.[21] Washington's road to war would clearly put Moscow "between Iraq and a hard place," as it were, and force Moscow precisely to make the choice that it had been trying so hard to avoid, that between a fruitless isolation and a dangerous confrontation.

French and German leadership of the international antiwar party provided diplomatic cover for Putin. While Russia now opposed Washington, it did so by siding with two of America's most important allies. The prospect of a tripartite Franco-German-Russian coalition seemed to be an acceptable second-best alternative to the Russian-American partnership that Putin had gambled on and lost the previous year.

Operationally, this stance meant that the Russians supported the French in crafting a two-stage process before the UN Security Council could authorize the war. The French, Germans, and Russians insisted that the United States could not go to war simply because Hussein was impeding UN arms inspectors. Instead, they insisted, the UN Security Council specifically had to approve the war before Washington could take military action. The Bush administration rejected this view, arguing that any evidence of Hussein's noncompliance with long-standing UN demands for unconditional cooperation with weapons inspectors itself justified a war.

In a last-ditch effort to stop the Americans, Putin made a dramatic dash to Paris in February 2003 for an antiwar summit with Jacques Chirac and Gerhard Schroeder. Their meeting resulted in a joint Franco-German-Russian statement that opposed war without specific authorization from the Security Council and gave a ringing endorsement of Russia's renewed preference for a multipolar world.

Interviewed on French television, Putin dramatically declared,

> [The] main thing is that France and Russia have common approaches to constructing the future edifice of international security. As we believe here in Russia, and as the French President Chirac believes, the future edifice of world security must be based on a multipolar world. I am absolutely confident that the world will be predictable and stable only if it is multipolar.[22]

Putin took one last initiative in order to forestall the coming war in Iraq. On the evening of March 17, 2003, Putin summoned former prime minister Yevgeny Primakov, who had known Saddam Hussein for decades. The next morning Primakov arrived in Iraq with a personal message from Putin to the Iraqi dictator. In a tense face-to-face meeting, Primakov verbally relayed Putin's message to Hussein: "If you love your people and your country, if you want to save your people and country from inevitable harm, you should resign as President of Iraq." Primakov emphasized that it was Putin's personal message, that it was a serious proposal, and that if Hussein accepted it, it would change his entire life, implying he would have a comfortable exile in Russia. According to Primakov, Hussein declined, replying that the Americans had tried to get rid of him before, during the Gulf War, but after much ado, they had simply given up and left.[23]

In the end, of course, Saddam Hussein played into the Americans' hands. The United States had the power to get its way and simply bypassed the UN Security Council and therewith the French, Germans, and Russians on the road to Baghdad. At the same time, Putin's collaboration with the Germans and especially the French took the sting out of his disagreement with Washington. As U.S. national security adviser Condoleezza Rice famously said later, the United States would "punish France, ignore Germany and forgive Russia."[24]

More disappointing to Putin than failing to prevent the Americans from going to war was the rapid realization that the antiwar entente with Paris and Berlin was just a one-time tactical alignment of short-term interests and not the foundation of an alternative international system. Before long, Paris and Berlin would be approving the further expansion of NATO to include the former Soviet republics of Estonia, Latvia, and Lithuania. Moreover, and in implicit confirmation of the hopelessness of their cause, the Russian, German, and French governments instructed their UN Security Council representatives on May 22, 2003, to vote to authorize the United States and Great Britain to administer Iraq. By August, the three recognized the Iraqi Governing Council established by Washington.

The Iraq War and its immediate aftermath underscored the precariousness of Putin's foreign policy position. Realistically mindful of the constraints on Russian power, Putin had hoped to leverage a privileged security relationship with Washington after the terror attacks of September 11, 2001, during Washington's hour of need. When this ambitious but calculated gamble failed, as became clear within the year, Putin then sought to work with two of Washington's leading allies, France and Germany, to find a substitute that, nevertheless, would anchor Russia firmly in the Western camp. This bid failed as well, as there was simply nothing that Russia could offer Berlin or Paris to compensate for the dense network of their interlocking economic, political, and security arrangements with the United States. All the while, as the limits of Russia's external influence were being painfully exposed, the Western world, driven by the United States, was expanding its security borders right up to Russia's frontiers. The West's collaboration with political forces in Russia's borderlands threatened to isolate Russia even further and perhaps posed a risk to Putin's power in Russia itself.

PUTIN'S RUSSIA AND THE "POST-SOVIET SPACE"

Long before Putin became Russia's president, Boris Yeltsin's government was grappling with the entirely novel phenomenon of establishing relations with the former Soviet provinces as a matter of foreign policy instead of domestic political management. Overnight, some 25 million ethnic Russians found themselves outside of formal Russian jurisdiction as residents, if not always citizens, of the newly independent post-Soviet states. Huge, portentous, and entirely unexpected issues had to be resolved as part of the gigantic Soviet "divorce settlement." Officials in Moscow needed to remove thousands of strategic nuclear weapons located in Belarus, Kazakhstan, and Ukraine to Russia. They had to resolve tensions and armed conflict in ethnically mixed regions throughout the Russian periphery and most dramatically within Russia itself in Chechnya. They also faced the challenge of establishing meaningful security frontiers in the wake of the Soviet collapse. Moreover, the Russian government had to react to these multiple and often mutually reinforcing problems in the context of a sharp decline in the Russian state's capacity to deal with them and a corresponding increase in the wealth, power, and reach of the United States and its NATO partners along Russia's western borderlands in Europe.

Russia's foreign and national security elites quickly coined a term that reflected their conviction that the post-Soviet countries of the Commonwealth of Independent States (CIS) occupied a unique place among Moscow's external relationships, "the near abroad," that is, neither truly domestic nor completely foreign. The intense relations throughout the CIS region meant (to Russian officials) that the corpus of international law could not be applied to Russian-CIS relations without significant modification. They resolved that Russia required special relationships with their "near abroad" neighbors.

This view was passed on intact from the Yeltsin to the Putin administration. What differed under Putin was the surge in Russian power, made possible by the rise of world energy prices after 1999. Now possessing greater capabilities, the Putin administration sought to establish post-Soviet Russia as the center of geopolitical gravity in central Eurasia. In this context, a series of events occurred between December 2003 and December 2004 that alarmed the Putin government: popular elections saw anti-Russian governments rise to power in key neighboring states. In Ukraine and Georgia, leaders who were eager to join NATO assumed office. In the case of Georgia, Putin's government tried to isolate Georgia economically. When that tactic did not work, in August 2008 Putin deployed the Russian Army to promote the secession of the Georgian provinces of South Ossetia and Abkhazia. He wanted to demonstrate that the path to the realization of Georgia's external interests ran through Moscow, not Washington. In doing so, Putin wanted to draw a line against further NATO expansion that included Ukraine as well.

DEALING AND MISDEALING WITH UKRAINE, 2004–2009

Most Russian policy elites, including Putin and his entourage, harbor no illusions that Ukraine either should or could be reincorporated into a Russian unitary state. At the same time, they are convinced that Russia's international status as well as its concrete economic and security interests require that at a minimum Ukraine not join a hostile alliance and at a maximum that Ukraine accept that its key international relationships be transacted through Moscow. Delegitimizing Ukrainian sovereignty has been a frequent resort of Russian politicians wanting to isolate Ukraine from developing its relations with the West. Putin employed this strategy directly with President Bush, telling him at the NATO summit meeting in Bucharest in April 2008, "Ukraine is not a real country."[25] Putin's remark to Bush, while crude, reflects a general Russian conviction that the separation from Russia of the historical Russian Empire's borderlands–Ukraine most of all–is abnormal, unfortunate, and temporary.[26] In Russia's view, while Ukraine might remain formally independent, it should coordinate its foreign policy and national security strategies with Moscow.

The Ukrainian presidential election cycle of late 2004–October 31, November 21, and December 26–represented a major opportunity and ultimately a deeply personal humiliation for Putin, as he intervened dramatically, publicly, and unsuccessfully to seat a pro-Russian candidate as Ukraine's head of state. Putin's preferred choice, Viktor Yanukovich, was the political heir of outgoing Ukrainian president Leonid Kuchma, who believed that the "Europeanization" of Ukraine should not come at the expense of Kiev's relations with Moscow. Putin's bête noir was candidate Viktor Yushchenko, whose second wife–daughter of anti-Soviet Ukrainian émigrés–was an American citizen and had once worked for the U.S. State Department. Yushchenko drew his support especially from western Ukraine, where anti-Russian sentiment ran strongest. Yushchenko stood for Ukraine's integration with the European Union and even NATO, whatever Moscow might think of it.

Putin understandably preferred that the pro-Russian candidate win the election, and he threw the impressive resources of the Russian government, whose coffers were now swelling with oil and gas revenues, behind Yanukovich's candidacy. Millions of dollars of Russian money were funneled Yanukovich's way, and Russian state television broadcast incessant pro-Yanukovich propaganda into Ukraine, where most citizens understood Russian easily. Putin himself made several dramatic visits to Ukraine in direct support of Yanukovich's candidacy, suggesting the benefits that would accrue to Ukraine with a close association with Moscow. For instance, in August 2004, Moscow signed a five-year gas contract with Kiev that entitled the Ukrainian government to purchase natural gas from Gazprom at $50 per 1,000 cubic meters, or less than a quarter of the price that the company was then fetching from Western European customers. The contract also committed Moscow to supply all of Ukraine's natural gas needs through 2009.[27]

Most visibly, on October 28, 2004, three days before the first, multi-candidate election round, Putin visited Ukraine in clear support of Yanukovich's candidacy. In a highly publicized interview to the three main Ukrainian television stations, Putin noted that he had invited Yanukovich as a personal guest to his birthday party earlier in the month. Then he explicitly endorsed Yanukovich's economic policy and implied an easing of cross-border travel between Ukraine and Russia in the event of Yanukovich's election. This matter was of great importance to millions of Ukrainian citizens who had family members and business dealings in Russia.[28]

Yushchenko's campaign, meanwhile, was strongly supported by foreign forces. Political activists from Georgia, who had just helped elect the anti-Russian Mikheil Saakashvili president, came to Ukraine to support the pro-Western and (they imagined) anti-Russian Yushchenko. (In November 2006, Yushchenko would become godfather to Saakashvili's youngest son.[29]) Ukrainian émigrés in Western Europe and especially Canada, who saw an opportunity to legitimize by electoral means Ukraine's exit from Russia's orbit, also assisted Yushchenko's campaign. Moreover, thousands of election officials from Western Europe and North America monitored the entire election campaign. As it turned out, anti-Russian émigrés from the Ukrainian diaspora were very well represented in these formally neutral organizations.[30]

Most dramatically, Yushchenko, a handsome and dashing figure who many in the country felt exuded a charismatic charm, suddenly fell ill in early

September 2004 with a disease that disfigured and then partially paralyzed his face. Eventually, Yushchenko was flown to Vienna, where doctors from the University of Virginia organized an intervention unit that established that a dioxin-based toxin had been introduced into Yushchenko's body. It produced the deformation of his face, as well as abdominal pains, cutaneous inflammation of his chest and face, digestive tract ulcers, and swelling of his liver, pancreas, and intestines. The concentration of dioxin in Yushchenko's blood was six thousand times higher than normal.[31]

Many in and outside the country thought that they detected the traces of a classic KGB operation, with a specific political objective. The object, in this view, was almost certainly not to kill Yushchenko–otherwise, ricin could just as easily have been employed–but to disable him during the campaign and leave the field clear for Moscow's man, Yanukovich. The logic? Had Yushchenko died, his probable replacement would have been Ukrainian nationalist Yulia Timoshenko. At the time, Moscow feared her candidacy even more than it did Yushchenko's.

Ukrainian president Viktor Yushchenko and Putin smile as they meet in Moscow's Kremlin (January 24, 2005). (Note the scars on Yushchenko's face from severe dioxin poisoning.)
Sergei Karpukhin/Reuters/Corbis

Whatever the precise explanation, Yushchenko's partial recovery from the dioxin attack and the all-too-plausible hand of the Russian secret services, or individuals in league with them, lent added energy to his presidential campaign.[32] To Moscow's astonishment and humiliation, Yushchenko prevailed in what amounted to a replay of the Serbian elections in the fall of 2000: international monitors exposed falsified election results and forced new elections, resulting in the installation of the opposition candidate.

The initial results showed a narrow plurality for Yushchenko (39.9 percent versus 39.3 percent for Yanukovich) in the first round of elections held on October 31, 2004. Since no candidate received a majority, a runoff round was held on November 21, in which Yanukovich claimed a modest but decisive majority over Yushchenko (49.5 percent versus 46.6 percent). Systematic analysis of exit polls, however, revealed that, in fact, Yushchenko should have been proclaimed the victor. European and North American election monitors legitimized charges of chicanery, and the news provoked massive demonstrations in Kiev and huge crowds occupied central Kiev for weeks on end. Intense negotiations within the Ukrainian government resulted in an agreement to hold new elections on December 26, which Yushchenko won decisively, 52 to 44 percent. Putin's government was shocked and humiliated. It had intervened publicly and dramatically in the Ukrainian election and lost.

In a doubling of his bet against Yushchenko, Putin later played a harsh energy card. Citing payments arrears and the need for market-clearing prices for Russian natural gas, Gazprom cut off the gas supplies to Ukraine in the dead of winter on January 1, 2006. Putin personally authorized this action.[33] His objectives were clear: to encourage the overthrow of Yushchenko, to control Ukraine's pipeline network in exchange for forgiveness of its energy debt to Russia, and to isolate Ukraine diplomatically in Europe.[34]

Once again, Putin overplayed his hand, as the Ukrainians in turn cut off the transit through Ukraine of Russian gas to Western Europe.[35] This move caused the immediate and direct intervention by the European Union and the resumption of Russian gas flows to Ukraine within three days. Ironically, Putin elicited the opposite of what he had intended. Instead of isolating Ukraine and demonstrating to its leaders that the only foreign policy option was to coordinate with Moscow, his action led to the European Union's intervention, which showed that Ukraine's energy security was a matter of importance to all of Europe and not just Russia. Moreover, the Ukrainians continued to pay a price for Russian natural gas that was well below that charged to Gazprom's Western European customers.

Remarkably, Putin, as prime minister, attempted the same maneuver in January 2009, citing as justification pricing disputes and alleged Ukrainian siphoning of Russian natural gas deliveries to Europe. This time, the Ukrainians were prepared, as they had built up a sufficient reserve supply of natural gas to see them through April. Inasmuch as this dispute lasted more than two weeks, Gazprom lost nearly $2 billion in revenues at a time of sharply declining energy prices. Once again, Putin failed to induce the Ukrainians to pay market-clearing prices. And while this time Ukraine, too, came under European criticism for double-dealing with Moscow, the crisis seriously damaged Russia's reputation as a reliable supplier to Western Europe. This dispute provoked a serious search for long-term alternatives to overdependence on Russian natural gas supplies. Slovakia, for instance, restarted a Chernobyl-type nuclear reactor that the European Union had forced it to close, while serious discussions began in Sweden, Germany, and Italy about revisiting those countries' renunciation of nuclear power, taken in the aftermath of the 1986 Chernobyl nuclear disaster. (Germany and Italy later reversed course after the Japanese nuclear disaster of March 2011.) Europeans also explored purchasing large quantities of liquefied natural gas, which can be shipped by ocean-going tankers from sources around the world, thereby bypassing Russia. Finally, a number of European states began intensively investigating revolutionary new ways to extract natural gas from shale rock. Developed in the United States and Canada, such techniques have the potential to expand European gas production dramatically and reduce dependence on Russian natural gas deliveries.

Time and again in relations with Ukraine, Putin's government seemed incapable of elementary scenario planning. Putin assumed that he could deal with the government of sovereign Ukraine as he had handled so many troublesome problems and individuals within Russia, that is, through the overwhelming application of superior power resources. During three successive crises, each of Russia's making, Putin failed to appreciate the subtleties of exercising influence under conditions of complex interdependence. Instead of setting up Ukraine for an easy checkmate, Putin had himself been maneuvered into a multilevel chess game of indefinite duration. The successive crises of 2004–2009 suggest that the extremely centralized "vertical [distribution] of power" that Putin had established was failing in some elementary functions of strategic planning (ironically, the subject of Putin's candidate's thesis). Were Putin's subordinates, leery of seeming to cross their boss, providing him with a distorted and incomplete picture of Ukrainian realities, or was Putin himself in part blinded by an obsession with bringing Ukraine to heel? The evidence to date supports both hypotheses.

KYRGYZSTAN PLAYS THE FIELD

Putin encountered significant difficulties in exercising Russian influence even in much smaller post-Soviet states like Kyrgyzstan, where in 2001 Putin had permitted the establishment of U.S. military bases in connection with the war in Afghanistan. The Americans, who had promised Putin that their bases in Central Asia would be temporary, seemed in no hurry to vacate the Manas Air Base, which had become a major assembling point for military transit flights into Afghanistan. Putin's government had no interest in seeing the United States establish permanent military bases throughout Central Asia. By late 2005, for instance, the United States was compelled to vacate the Karshi-Khanabad Air Base in Uzbekistan, only to see a long-term military basing deal signed between Moscow and Tashkent.

By February 2009, the Barack Obama administration learned with evident displeasure that the United States soon might have to evacuate its major military facility in Kyrgyzstan. It quickly transpired during the Kyrgyz president's visit to Moscow that month that Putin's government had offered the cash-strapped Kyrgyz authorities $150 million in direct foreign assistance and a $2 billion credit on favorable terms, or twice the amount of the Kyrgyz government's annual budget. Putin wanted Washington to acknowledge that it could operate on post-Soviet space only on terms agreed by Moscow.

By summer 2009, however, the tables had been partially turned. The Kyrgyz government had been playing Moscow and Washington against each other all along in order to obtain the highest price for its allegiance. Having pocketed $450 million in Russian aid and credits, the Kyrgyz authorities induced the U.S. government to triple the price for the use of the Manas Air Base (to $60 million per year, in addition to $50 million in direct aid). In late June 2009, the Kyrgyz government agreed to renew the U.S. lease on the base. As Russian military analyst Alexander Golts put it, "A game of chance has developed in the post-Soviet space: Who can swindle the Kremlin in the coolest way?"[36]

Moscow, though outraged, was powerless to annul the deal. In a sign of the dilemmas and constraints informing Russian diplomacy, Putin's government agreed for the first time to allow the use of Russian airspace for U.S. military aircraft to transport military supplies to Afghanistan.[37] Putin, after all, had no interest in seeing another Taliban victory on the old Soviet border. At the same time, Russia quickly signed an agreement with the Kyrgyz government to give Russia a twenty-year lease on a second military base in the country. Thus, Kyrgyzstan and other third parties used the ongoing geopolitical competition between Washington and Moscow to play each off against the other, as happened so often in the third world during the Cold War. Moscow's exclusive diplomatic influence in the region was far from given.

SUMMING UP

Putin largely succeeded in asserting the priority of Russia's economic and security interests along the southern periphery of the former Soviet Union. In Central Asia, by pressuring or inducing local governments to exchange American for Russian military bases in Uzbekistan and negotiating the exclusive export of natural gas through Moscow's pipeline network in Kazakhstan and Turkmenistan, he contained the penetration of American economic and military power. Further west, in the Caucasus, Putin consolidated Russia's influence over Armenia and smashed Georgia's armed forces, thereby underscoring his determination and capacity to enforce Russia's writ in the region.

Still, the challenges are formidable and the costs considerable. In Kyrgyzstan, the government in Bishkek played Russia off against the United States for the highest bid, and Washington kept its military base. In the Baltic region, Estonia, Latvia, and Lithuania never joined the CIS and instead integrated themselves into the European Union and NATO. In Ukraine, a series of Russian interventions backfired and inspired even more assiduous efforts in Kiev to escape from Moscow's influence.

Although Putin has asserted Russia's authority, he has not consolidated Russian hegemony anywhere in the post-Soviet region. While he has limited Western influence and contained American power in parts of the near abroad, Russia's post-Soviet neighbors retain some room for maneuver. Nowhere throughout the post-Soviet region has Putin's Russia definitively consolidated Moscow's predominance. In the end, Russian influence is a matter of persuasion and inducement rather than command and compulsion. Even in Georgia, the Russians failed to obtain significant international recognition of the independence of South Ossetia and Abkhazia from Georgia. Not one post-Soviet state apart from Russia extended diplomatic recognition to them. And as Putin discovered, through painful trial and error, it was much more difficult to manipulate elections outside Russia than within. Sovereignty matters.

Putin has tried to revive Russian stature and power employing whatever means and capabilities he could harness. His initial foreign policy preference was for a partnership with the West. When these hopes were dashed, Putin then tried to use his nation's energy resources and mounting revenues to consolidate Russia's predominance throughout post-Soviet Eurasia. But this strategy failed in Russia's handling of its single most important neighbor, Ukraine. And once oil prices collapsed–dropping from $145 per barrel in July 2008 to $35 in December 2008–Putin faced a real dilemma. His political machine and his foreign policy depended on increasing revenues from oil, gas, and other raw materials. If they disappeared, what would be his legacy?

CONCLUSION:
TO 2012 AND BEYOND

"This is in no way stability; this is exhaustion after the Yeltsin years."
— Vladislav Surkov, deputy head of Putin's
Presidential Administration, 2003[1]

"Russia has almost no other infrastructure and industry except for those inherited from the Soviet Union."
— Russian economist Mikhail Delyagin, August 21, 2009[2]

When Vladimir Putin transferred his title as president to Dmitri Medvedev in May 2008, it seemed to most observers at home and abroad that Putin's model of Potemkin democracy—with its implicit exchange of economic performance for political conformity—had proven its worth. Unprecedented domestic prosperity and stability and heightened international status gave Putin's regime genuine popular legitimacy. His main task as prime minister seemed to be to supervise a smooth transition into the indefinite future.

Supporting this view, Medvedev was the beneficiary of arguably the best ten years in Russian history. Between 1999 and 2008, the Russian economy averaged 7 percent growth per year, attaining a high of 10 percent in 2000 and a low of 5.1 percent in 2001. Real disposable incomes nearly doubled despite a rate of consumer inflation above 10 percent per year throughout this period. Living standards now approached and in a number of respects exceeded those of the late Soviet period, before the economic collapse that began in 1989–

1990. Federal fiscal policy exhibited definite signs of sobriety as the revenues of the central government more than doubled, growing from a low of 11.4 percent of Russian GDP in 1998, the last full year before Putin assumed power, to 24 percent of a much larger GDP by 2007. Government expenditures grew more moderately, ranging from 14.6 percent to 19 percent of GDP throughout this period, and culminated in budget surpluses from 4.4 percent to 7.5 percent of GDP between 2004 and 2007.[3] Dollar and euro reserves of the Russian Central Bank approached $600 billion, making them the third largest in the world. Reserve and stabilization funds had been established amounting to more than $200 billion.[4] Further, the war in Chechnya seemed to be won, and just as important, the outside world did not contest Russian policy in the province. There had been no large-scale terrorist attack in Russia since the horrible Beslan school siege in September 2004.

Putin had also established a more solid international footing for Russia than had his predecessor, Boris Yeltsin. The financial solvency of the Russian government at home and abroad underscored the country's newfound freedom of action in world affairs. The U.S. and European governments recognized that they could not solve the world's energy equation without involving Russia. Western firms competed eagerly for Russian energy contracts even as Putin's government changed their terms dramatically in its favor. Throughout Central Asia, Putin had moved to limit U.S. freedom of action, and he made it clear that a solution to Iran's nuclear ambitions could not be reached without Russia's agreement. Putin's Russia was a Russia that could say no to the United States, a novel development for U.S. administrations that were accustomed to easy acquiescence from the Yeltsin and Gorbachev governments. The International Olympic Committee's decision to award the 2014 Winter Olympics to Russia symbolized the country's recent international recognition: Russia was a country that mattered again.

Not surprisingly, Russian policy elites now began to speak not just of Russia's recovery but also of its resurgence, which justified a major role for Russia in global economic councils. Some even mentioned the ruble as a supplementary reserve currency and mocked U.S. fiscal and trade deficits. But such bravura quickly evaporated when a succession of global shocks battered the Russian economy and called into question the sustainability of Putin's model of political-economic development.

CRISIS MANAGEMENT AND LOST OPPORTUNITIES

The first months of 2008 brought signs of economic troubles to come. The Russian housing market fell into recession, the inflation rate exceeded 13 percent, and the ruble continued to appreciate, rendering Russian domestic manufactures less competitive against foreign imports. But with the price of oil at $145 a barrel in July 2008, such problems seemed easy to manage. The alarm bell did not ring until after the Georgian-Russian five-day war in August. Within weeks, and before the onset of the global financial crisis in September and October, the Russian stock market lost 35 percent of its value and Russian capital fled the country. By October the stock market had lost 75 percent of its value.[5] Now faced with the collapse of U.S. credit markets and its global reverberations, the Russian government was confronted with a true emergency. While Russia had substantial financial reserves that would allow it to ride out the crisis for a time, those reserves—in the context of plummeting energy prices—could not last indefinitely without either the end of the global recession, the tapping of alternative sources of revenue at home, or serious cutbacks in governmental expenditures.

Almost immediately, Putin—who, as prime minister, was directly responsible for economic policy—took dramatic steps to staunch the outflow of funds. Expecting the Russian economy to contract by as much as 8 percent in 2009 (which it did), or a fifteen-point decline from the previous year, within two months Putin spent $200 billion, which was fully one-third of the government's dollar reserves, to prop up Russian banks and prevent a precipitous drop in the ruble's value. Nevertheless, the ruble continued to decline. Standard & Poor's downgraded the Russian government's debt rating to BBB, just one grade above junk status, for the first time since Putin came to power.[6] Putin then quickly moved a new budget through the Duma for 2009, one that was based on an average price of oil of $41 per barrel instead of the originally planned $95 price. Even under these draconian conditions, he acknowledged that government revenues would fall 42 percent and the government's budget would go into the red, with an 8 percent budget deficit.[7] Putin also cut taxes deeply on oil exports so as to encourage production in the face of the huge price drop.[8] By May 2009, underscoring the social and political dangers of the crisis, 38 percent of the Russian workforce was facing significant arrears in wages.[9]

Putin's rapid economic interventions, in which his government spent 12 percent of the country's GDP to prop up the economy, proved their worth in the short term.[10] Although the Russian economy contracted by 10 percent in the first half of 2009 and 7.9 percent for the year as a whole, the government remained solvent and the ruble did not collapse.[11] By contrast, the collapse of world oil prices in 1998 had triggered default and devaluation under Boris Yeltsin. Measured deficit spending and other stimulus measures had kept the fragile banking system intact, even while Putin put vital, long-term investment projects on indefinite hold. By mid-2009, the price of oil had stabilized around $70 per barrel, and the Russian economy appeared to be stable for the time being.

Putin understood that Russia could not deal with a crisis of this magnitude on its own. In January 2009, he attended the annual world economic conference in Davos, Switzerland, for the first time and issued a dramatic appeal for international cooperation to end the economic crisis in an address titled "We're All in the Same Boat." Putin took great pains to distance Russia from the Soviet Union in the minds of his audience, stressing that Russia would not revert to economic isolationism or totalitarian economics. Command-style economics, Putin said, in words reminiscent of his dissertation, "made the Soviet economy totally uncompetitive. This lesson cost us dearly. I am sure that nobody wants to see it repeated." At the same time, in a rebuke to Anglo-American market fundamentalism, Putin declared that blind faith in the virtues of the free market was as misleading as unbridled statism of the Soviet type. Speaking as a Keynesian advocate of well-regulated and managed markets, Putin underscored that intelligent and targeted management of the economic crisis by all governments, acting alone and in concert, was required.

Interestingly, Putin in Davos implicitly conceded a point that many of his critics had made: Russia had become a petrostate excessively dependent on energy exports for its prosperity and stability. The global economic crisis had "made the problems we had more evident," Putin said. He continued,

> They concern the excessive reliance on raw materials in exports and the economy in general and a weak financial market. The need to develop a number of fundamental market institutions, above all of a competitive environment, has become more acute. . . . [T]he declared [priority] is to effect a qualitative renewal of Russia in the next 10 to 12 years.[12]

In sum, while the Russian economy had grown substantially under Putin, it had not yet begun to develop into the more balanced and modern economy

Prime Minister Putin addresses the "Private Meeting of the Members of the International Business Council with Vladimir Putin" at the Annual Meeting of the World Economic Forum in Davos, Switzerland (January 29, 2009). Xinhua Press/Corbis

that Putin himself had for years said was necessary for the country's long-term health. How much of this enormous missed opportunity was Putin's responsibility?

Putin had been warned. Throughout his second term as president, a number of free-market economists who had initially supported Putin sharply criticized the state's expanding grip on the Russian economy and society. The most prominent among them, Andrei Illarionov, left the government at the end of 2005 and became a harsh critic of Putin's regime, declaring dramatically that Russia was no longer a free country. More alarming, Vladimir Milov, who had served as an energy adviser in Putin's first term, and liberal democrat and Yeltsin-era minister Boris Nemtsov penned a scathing indictment of Putin's system and identified key Putin allies with massive corruption and mismanagement. While Putin succeeded in suppressing the report (by restricting its sale to the one kiosk in Russia owned by the publisher), he would have been well advised to heed these harbingers of disagreeable news.

In their analysis, the substance of which, remarkably, was endorsed by Russian president Medvedev, Milov and Nemtsov emphasized that Russia's impressive economic growth was tied primarily to the rise in world energy prices.[13] They argued that in light of recent Chinese and even Indian growth rates, the energy boom should have sustained Russian growth rates nearly twice as high, between 10 to 15 percent per year instead of the actual 6 to 7 percent.[14] In effect, Milov and Nemtsov claimed that Putin's policies achieved much less for the Russian economy than had the simple rise in the price of fossil fuels. Moreover, they suggested that Putin's government had failed to exploit windfall energy prices to lay the foundations for the country's modernization. Few steps had been taken to implement structural reforms to make the economy less dependent in the long run on energy and raw materials. There had been no significant investment in transportation and other critical infrastructures or much effort to create viable public health, pension, and even military systems. While Russia had recovered from the effects of the Soviet collapse, it had not developed practices leading to self-sustaining and balanced economic growth and political accountability.

Growth in the absence of development, insisted Milov and Nemtsov, was the hallmark of the Putin years. Early liberal economic reforms were abandoned in the face of Putin's authoritarianism in the political field. The government became overly involved in business and succumbed to a pathological increase in corruption. The corruption, in turn, reinforced patterns of non-transparent decision making and diverted efforts to tackle problems that were fundamental to the country's prospects.[15]

This pattern of missed opportunities was most glaring in the alarming condition of Russia's transportation and industrial infrastructure. For instance, although it is impossible to reliably traverse the length of Russia by car or truck, and the only true world-class highway systems in Russia are the ring roads around Moscow and St. Petersburg, under Putin the amount of paved highways in Russia actually declined by 9 percent.[16] In 2009 the World Economic Forum ranked the quality of Russia's road system as 118th out of 133 countries evaluated, placing it alongside Mozambique and Burundi in this category.[17]

In the critical energy sphere, Russian oil production during the boom years has been driven mainly by intensively exploiting oil fields that were established during the late Soviet period rather than by investing in extensive exploration and new development of (extremely expensive) new fields in subarctic and Arctic Russia. While increasing production in the short term, the effect has been to accelerate the fields' depletion. As a result, by 2008 Russian oil production had begun to level off and even decline temporarily, hinting at an impending energy crisis within Russia if the country does not make a massive commitment to renewing its energy infrastructure. Incredibly, Russia has not built a single new oil refinery since the collapse of the Soviet Union.[18]

In effect, Putin exploited the decade-long energy boom to maximize short-term revenues at the expense of the long-term viability of Russia's energy system. In the process, untold billions of dollars were siphoned off in patently corrupt transactions. A priceless opportunity was lost to invest in the country's energy future as well as to lay the groundwork for diversifying the Russian economy away from such heavy reliance on raw materials exports. In this author's estimate, those charged with administering the energy system on the state's behalf have looted roughly half of Russia's income from oil and natural gas. Along these lines, James Harmon, former president of the Export-Import Bank of the United States, stated in December 2010 he had "never witnessed a state steal such a large amount from investors" as took place during the prosecution of Mikhail Khodorkovsky, former head of the Yukos energy firm.[19]

To give just one example of the extent of the mismanagement and corruption in the energy sector, when oil was fetching $145 per barrel in mid-2008, Russian energy analysts at ING, the Dutch investment house, calculated the break-even point for Russia's largest oil firm, Lukoil, at $80 per barrel.[20] Yet the costs of production probably did not exceed $20 per barrel. This gap of $65 per barrel between production costs and the break-even point—and in the absence of large-scale investment in energy infrastructure!—underscored the scope of incompetence and malfeasance that threatens Russia's energy future.[21] This is not simply a question of corruption. Russian oil and natural gas firms have been required by the government to sell their gas to domestic customers at a fraction of the world market price, at times as low as one-fifth the world price.[22] Such subsidies are a major element in the social support for Putin's political machine, yet at the same time they deprive the energy sector of massive revenues essential to long-term modernization.

PUTIN'S LEGACY

How is Vladimir Putin's historical legacy to be evaluated under these circumstances? Making such an appraisal is necessarily a tentative and risky enterprise;

as of the time of this writing (July 2011) Putin remains the most powerful politician in Russia, with evident ambitions to keep the reins of power for the indefinite future. For instance, when President Medvedev fired the powerful mayor of Moscow Yuri Luzhkov on September 28, 2010, he was replaced by Sergei Sobyanin, Putin's chief of staff.[23] Throughout the economic crisis, Medvedev ceded center stage to Putin. Even in foreign and security policy—where the Russian president is constitutionally superior to the prime minister—Putin intervened at critical moments to direct the course of events, as he did when he dramatically flew to the North Caucasus to supervise operations during the Georgia-Russia war in August 2008.[24] Thus, not only is the history of the Putin era necessarily incomplete; how one assesses Putin's historical legacy is certain to be affected by events yet to come.

On the positive side of the ledger, Putin stopped and reversed the crumbling of the Russian state, won the war in Chechnya, encouraged economic recovery after the calamitous post-Soviet decade, increased the country's international standing, and capably managed the threatening consequences of the global financial crisis and recession of 2008–2009. This record of accomplishment is considerable, whatever happens in the years to come. Thoughtful Russians, critics and supporters alike, concede the positive impact that Putin had at a time when the future of Russia itself seemed to be at stake.

Russian journalist Vladimir Solovyov, for instance, has argued that Putin is one of the few leaders in Russian history who, whether one approves of him or not, "succeeded in changing the country's direction." The centrifugal movement of Russia's government from the late Gorbachev period through the 1990s was replaced by the centripetal flow of power to the central government in Moscow.[25] Even critics, like Mikhail Gorbachev, who have disparaged Putin because of Russia's undoubted "democratic deficit" throughout his tenure in power have conceded that Putin made major contributions by stabilizing the country at a critical time in its history. "During his first term in office," wrote Gorbachev, "Putin succeeded in restoring stability and improving the governability of the country. In the process, he opened up new prospects to realize his program, which at the time I termed 'social democratic.'"[26]

At the same time, even strong Putin supporters admit that there are major defects in his political regime that constrain Russia's long-term prospects. Solovyov, in a generally sympathetic book-length portrayal, concluded that

Putin's aversion to open politics was harmful to Russia's interests. "One of the basic problems of Putin's government," Solovyov wrote,

> is the absolute non-transparency of decision-making, whether it be in the selection of personnel or in policy itself. The fact that people cannot understand the course of events . . . , of the decision-making process, of personnel policy and the method for selecting officials, is alarming. In Russia . . . , the portion of politics carried out in the public sphere is still immeasurably small. And this tendency needs to gradually fade into history.[27]

Secrecy and control, of course, are the stock in trade of those whom Putin has used to staff his government, above all the strong contingent of military and intelligence officials who make up his loyal base in the Presidential Administration and throughout the government. In building his government, Putin staffed it, understandably, with those who shared his vision of Russia's future and whose personal loyalty he did not question. In this way, Putin went a long way toward solving a problem that every leader, democratic or otherwise, faces: that is, he was able to induce the governmental bureaucracy to implement the policies that he endorsed. Consequently, Putin's administration was staffed over time predominantly either by those who had worked with him in Sobchak's mayoralty in St. Petersburg between 1990 and 1996 or by former colleagues from the intelligence and other military and paramilitary services.

The first group included a number of convinced free-market economists, often more interested in free markets than in free polities. The second group, with security officials, saw the Soviet Union's collapse as the "greatest geopolitical tragedy of the twentieth century," as Putin put it in 2005. Further, they believed that command by the state—in the economy as in the political system— was the key to Russia's resurgence. In most respects, they were also following Putin's lead: Putin has chosen the certainties of command over the promises of liberty in almost every instance where he has had a choice. He correctly perceived that after the trauma of the Gorbachev and Yeltsin years, most Russians were yearning for order, and as far as most Russians have been concerned, Putin has provided it. For them, Putin's Russia is a country that, as Russian political scientist Boris Mazo has put it, "has normal, positive development, without revolutions, without leaps and crashes, without periodic confiscation and redistribution of property."[28] As a result, Putin's personal popularity has remained in the stratosphere throughout a decade in power, ranging between 68 and 87 percent.[29] In this regard, in late 2010 *The Economist* Intelligence Unit concluded that "most Russians appear unperturbed by the trend toward authoritarianism" that has characterized Putin's rule.[30]

It was Putin's fate to attempt the rebuilding of the Russian state in a time of war and terrorism at home. He assumed power in 1999 determined to restore the power and prestige of the Russian state and in the process lay the foundations for Russia's post-Soviet modernization. Yet arguably, the ways in which Putin reestablished state authority seriously hindered Russia's chances for modernization. Throughout his presidency, he tended to see the main danger to Russia as stemming from disintegration rather than stagnation.[31] Putin thus resolved the tension between his intellectual grasp of the requirements of reform and his emotional commitment to order and control by embracing control at the expense of reform. Relatedly, he staffed his administration increasingly with military and paramilitary personnel who shared his proclivity for command and control. As a result, he constructed a regime that has skillfully manipulated political power but seems incapable of managing many of the country's critical longer-term challenges.

Putin inherited many challenges upon taking power in 1999 and he clearly recognized what they were, but they were no closer to resolution a decade later than they had been at the outset. For instance, in 2006 Putin declared that Russia faced a demographic emergency that was the country's most urgent challenge; yet in March 2011, the CIA reported life expectancy for Russian males at the shockingly low level of 59.8 years, or a dozen years fewer than in countries like China and Turkey. Given that male life expectancy in the city of Moscow was sixty-nine years, the situation was obviously worse in most of the rest of the country, thus underscoring the extremely unbalanced economic and social development of the Putin years.

Relatedly, high death rates and low birth rates prefigure a likely 23 percent decrease in the country's population by 2050, from 140 million in 2009 to 110 million. Such a drastic and unprecedented reduction will have huge constraining effects on military recruitment (where more than one-third of the draftees are already rejected on health grounds), the country's rudimentary social security system, and the productivity of the labor force, which in 2009 stood at just one-fourth to one-third of the level in the United States.[32] To make matters worse, by 2025, according to Rosstat, the official Russian statistics bureau, the working-age population will decline by nearly 15 million people.[33] This drop portends a major economic crisis in the medium term, as Russia's economy in 2009 was already the only major one in which production in the manufacturing sector had not increased in the past two decades.[34]

Such facts bode especially ill for the more than 450 single-company towns throughout Russia—constituting one-fourth of the urban population—whose entire socioeconomic life depends on the fate of their respective firms, which are noncompetitive on the free market even in good economic times. The banking system remained severely undercapitalized, and in spite of a substantial recovery of the agricultural sector, the value of Russia's food imports in 2008 was thrice that of its food exports, with the country importing nearly half of its food annually. This deficit placed Russia in the company of Japan, with a small fraction of Russia's arable land, as the only net food importers among the major industrialized countries.[35]

Such deeply rooted social, economic, and demographic trends indicated that for all of Putin's undoubted accomplishments, he had yet to develop a model of political economy that represented a clear break with the Soviet legacy of stunted modernization. Perhaps under the circumstances he could not do much more than stop the rot and channel part of the energy bonanza toward the state's coffers. In any event, the emergence of Russia from under the rubble of the Soviet era and its painful aftermath was always likely to be a matter of generations and not terms of office of particular political leaders.

Still, after a decade in power, Putin seemed at a loss as to how to move the Russian nation toward the Europeanized version of modernity that continues to inspire him. On the one hand, his government rests heavily in the hands of a military and paramilitary elite—led by Deputy Prime Minister Igor Sechin—that is reluctant to devolve power to economic and social forces outside the state's purview. Where control and efficiency come into conflict, this elite embraces control. On the other hand, the resulting confluence of politics and economics at the apex of Putin's system has helped to fuel a syndrome of corruption that has led a competing faction of economic technocrats—championed by Putin's deputy chief of staff Vladislav Surkov and finance minister Aleksei Kudrin—to oppose large-scale investment in vital infrastructure projects. They argue that such funds would be wasted in corruption, provoking a new bout of inflation without corresponding benefits in higher future productivity. Considerations of economic efficiency, in this view, should prevail over the urge for bureaucratic control.

These tensions within Putin's machine were clearly illustrated with the appearance of two plans for economic modernization that were being elaborated in spring 2011. One plan, entitled "Strategy for 2012," was formulated by the Institute of Contemporary Development and connected to President Medvedev's office. This document argued that Russia's future economic development depended on implementing major economic and political reforms, requiring a large reduction in the government's grip on the economy and the introduction of genuine political pluralism. The other plan, called "Strategy for 2020," was originally commissioned by Putin in 2008 and called for an entirely different program, one focused on preserving the central role of the state in the economy and the "managed democracy" of the Putin era.[36] It was difficult to see, given Putin's enduring grip on the Russian political system, where the impetus for major structural transformation might come from. More to the point, Russians themselves were now increasingly skeptical about the government's ability to bring about positive changes in the country. A Levada Center poll released in late March 2011 showed that 40 percent of Russians had no faith in Kremlin modernization plans, versus 23 percent who did. This is the largest percentage of skeptics since the Levada Center began polling on the subject.[37]

Here is the crux of the matter: In order for Russia to escape the orbit of the corrupt petrostate, Putin needs to break with central elements of the system that he has built. The most powerful forces in his administration fear transparency and open political and economic competition, while the lawyers and economists who remain—and who claim to see their spokesman in President Medvedev—are skeptical that the economy can be transformed without reducing the state's grip on the economy. Moreover, the severe underdevelopment of small- and medium-size businesses in Russia—stable at a low level of 17 percent of all businesses throughout the Putin years—means that Russian society is too amorphous and weak either to monitor the workings of the government or to become its partner in a program of economic and political transformation.[38] The political foundations for liberalization are thus weak, while the forces of the status quo appear bound up within a closed circle of Potemkin democracy and a dependency on receipts from raw materials. To date, Putin has sought to balance the factions of order and development, to the benefit of the former and at the cost of the latter. It remains to be seen whether Putin or others can adapt the "Putin machine" to stimulate Russia's transformation without provoking a fateful loss of political control. No doubt, when more definitive histories of the

Putin era are written, Putin's success or failure in this enterprise will constitute a major component of his historical reputation.

FOREIGN POLICY

The choices that Putin made in Russian foreign policy, especially after the failure of his openings toward the United States and Western Europe between 2001 and 2003, also seemed to limit the short-term chances for modernizing the country. Putin wanted to deal with the West from a position of equality, but Russia's economic, military, geopolitical, and demographic realities belied such hopes. Much the same was true of Russia's relations with communist China, whose gross GDP exceeded Russia's fivefold and whose population along its eastern borderlands with Russia exceeded by ten times the population on the Russian side. At the same time, Putin wanted Russia to become the geopolitical fulcrum of the post-Soviet territories of central Eurasia so that he could exploit its energy predominance to leverage diplomatic and national security control. Yet even here, while achieving certain successes, Putin struggled mightily to contain the extension of Western and especially U.S. influence.

Putin refused to allow Russia to become a "peripheral" adjunct of either the Western world or of China, but he was unable to establish Russia as the center of its own geopolitical universe of post-Soviet states. Yet Russian economic and especially demographic trends cannot sustain Russia's claim to great power status. Nor does Russia wield much in the way of "soft" power assets—cultural sway, shared values, and so forth—that might induce many of its neighbors to voluntarily accept Russian leadership. When Russia resorts instead to using "hard" power—cutting off gas supplies, imposing economic sanctions, and taking military action—it has tended to encourage its neighbors to seek security in the protection of NATO and the United States.

The syndrome of asserting Russia's great-power claims without the resources to back them up was shown in an economic initiative in June 2009 that amazed Putin's European and U.S. counterparts. That month Putin announced, after public assurances by President Medvedev to the contrary, that Russia was withdrawing its application for admission to the World Trade Organization (WTO). Its membership, if its terms were taken seriously, would have required the comprehensive liberalization of the Russian economic and legal system. Instead, Putin declared, Russia would resubmit an application later but only as part of a customs union with Belarus and Kazakhstan (neither of which were WTO members, either). Such an initiative was without precedent in the organization's history and had little chance of being honored. After all, every EU member state had first been a member of the WTO before the EU itself was granted admission.

Four months later, in October 2009, Putin's government backed down after the WTO flatly rejected a joint Russia-Kazakhstan-Belarus entry into the organization.[39] Still, the episode underscored Putin's resistance, not to profitable relations with the West but to integration into the West—which dominates the WTO's agenda and values—*if* such integration would jeopardize the chances for Russian predominance throughout post-Soviet Eurasia. In a strategy that is consistent with his thinking since his days at the St. Petersburg Mining Institute, Putin has evidently calculated that Russia can leverage its claim to great-power status on the basis of its energy production and reserves. This, in effect, requires freedom of action from WTO rules, which prohibit the type of political exploitation of trade dependencies that Putin has deployed against Ukraine and Georgia. Yet even if the daunting challenges facing the Russian energy sector's long-term development are overcome, without fundamental changes in Russia's legal and political system, the petrostate model of stunted economic and political development would only be reinforced. This situation, in turn, would do little more than cement Russia's position as the core of a marginalized ghetto in the global political economy, thereby thwarting Putin's expressed desires for Russia's comprehensive modernization and its reestablishment as a great power.

Ironically, Russia's prospects for joining the WTO in the near future came to depend on Georgia consenting to Russian entry. Under the WTO's unit veto rules, Georgia—a WTO member—can block Russia's admission. After the 2008 war with Russia, the Georgian government was not eager for Russia to join and affixed a series of political conditions—concerning the status of Abkhazia and South Ossetia and the presence of Russian troops there—to Russia entering the trade body. In practice, Russia's prospects came to depend on whether the United States could provide sufficient economic inducements to, and diplomatic pressure on, Georgia to lift its opposition. Russia's global economic plans thus became a hostage to its ambitions for hegemony in post-Soviet Eurasia.[40]

But what if Russia's real choice was not *whether* to belong to somebody else's periphery but rather *which* periphery to join? In that case, Russia would have to choose, in effect, between the West *or* China, or it would mortgage its future to irreversible decline. Its choice of international orientation also entails a fundamental choice of internal direction: liberal modernization along Western lines or authoritarian modernization along Chinese lines. After twelve years of Putin's rule, which his defenders claimed justified a strategy of "authoritarian modernization," Russia seemed stuck in a twilight zone of authoritarian government without significant modernization. And after nearly three years of rule by the Putin-Medvedev "tandem," as *The Economist* Intelligence Unit concluded in late 2010, "there [had] been no fundamental reforms" in Russian politics or economics.[41]

The question may seem provocative, but after more than a decade in office—and in the absence of international partners sharing his vision of Russia's future—Putin seemed unable to elaborate an international strategy that corresponded to the country's pressing material interests while also satisfying its enormous desire for international respect.[42]

IN CLOSING

While Putin has established an authoritarian political regime with a democratic institutional veneer, his Potemkin democracy is a far cry from the Soviet Union even at its most liberal. Private property is widespread and its forms are respected even when, as is often the case, industrial and natural resource magnates need to coordinate their business practices with the Kremlin. Russians have the freedom to travel abroad and millions do so each year, almost all of them returning home (so contrary in both respects to Soviet-era practices). Freedom of religion is mainly observed in practice, with restrictions confined to proselytizing Western sects. And so long as Putin's power is not directly challenged, information flows freely in Russia for those interested in obtaining it, as the source base for this book illustrates. Even though the state controls the national television stations, in striking contrast to China, in Putin's Russia the Internet is not censored. In foreign affairs, Russia has no ideologically based conflicts with the outside world and has pursued a mainly pragmatic diplomacy, not always successful, aimed at maximizing Russian revenues and minimizing Russia's enemies. Moreover, in the wake of the 2008–2009 global economic crisis that Putin's government had weathered, the Russian economy began growing again, at 3.7 percent in 2010 and at a projected 4.3 percent for 2011.[43]

In this context, Russian optimists, such as political scientist Dmitri Trenin (himself often a Putin critic), see the Putin years as confirming the irreversibility of Russia's exit from the Soviet orbit and as laying the groundwork for Russia's long-term evolution along European lines. A continuation of widespread private property development and direct exposure to the West for another generation will, in his view, create the social foundations for a more balanced relationship between the state and society.[44] Trenin's view, while plausible, overlooks the possibility that Putin may have succeeded all too well and has created a self-perpetuating bureaucratic regime that at times resembles the late Leonid Brezhnev period in its reliance on high energy prices and in its resistance to structural reform of either the economy or the polity. Moreover, in light of Putin's successful stifling of legitimate political opposition—which has weakened an already fragile democratic camp—the alternatives to Putin's system in the short run are much more likely to be among the xenophobic, chauvinist, and anti-Semitic Right, not the liberal- or social-democratic Left.

In the immediate future, Putin's reputation will hinge on whether he can navigate Russia through the global economic storm on the basis of the authoritarian political machine that he has created. Barring another prolonged collapse of global energy prices, he may well succeed in this venture. Given the implosion of the economy amid similar conditions under both Yeltsin and Gorbachev, this would be a considerable accomplishment.

In the longer run, Putin may also be fairly judged by whether his system allows Russia to evolve toward a form of constitutional order that allows for a meaningful rule of law in which political interests are involved and that makes political succession something more than the current plaything of obscure court politics. Apart from their intrinsic political value, such steps are prerequisites to constraining the widespread corruption and illegality that weigh so heavily on Russia's economic prospects. After twelve years of Putin in power, this change was not on the political horizon. For instance, in September 2009, Putin declared that he and his protégé, Medvedev, would decide who runs for president in 2012, when Putin would be just fifty-nine years old. President Medvedev himself then stated publicly that he and Putin might even swap positions. In light of a constitutional amendment that Putin hastily passed in December 2008 extending the presidential term from four years to six years, Putin would then be eligible to serve twelve more years as president, or until 2024. Even were he not to run again, the choice is his and his alone. Russia remains a government of men, not of laws.

Putin on vacation in southwestern Siberia (summer 2008). Note the baptismal cross around his neck that he has never taken off in public. Used by permission of the website of the President of the Russian Federation, www.kremlin.ru.

In this respect, Putin failed to live up to the vision expressed by his teacher, mentor, and political godfather, Anatoly Sobchak. Writing in the early summer of 1999, half a year before his death and shortly before Putin's appointment as prime minister, Sobchak pondered Boris Yeltsin's legacy and the challenges facing his successor. Sobchak wrote that Yeltsin's Russia was a country of half measures: a semi-democratic, semi-market, and semi-legal approach to government, with the single exception of the full-blown rule of the bureaucracy. Whoever succeeded Yeltsin, Sobchak prophesied, would "face the incredibly complicated, inhumanly difficult task of moving the country out of this 'half-way house,' that is, to leave behind the condition of bureaucratic semi-democracy in favor of a democratic state based on the rule of law."[45] Sobchak, a fearless advocate of equal justice under law, would no doubt have been shocked that Russia had moved even closer to a state of "legal nihilism" after twelve years of his protégé Putin's rule.[46]

NOTES

Introduction

1. Alfred B. Evans Jr. interview by German television stations ARD and ZDF with Vladimir Putin, *Power and Ideology: Vladimir Putin and the Russian Political System*, Carl Beck Papers, no. 1902 (Pittsburgh, PA: University of Pittsburgh, Center for Russian and East European Studies, 2008), 5.
2. Wm. Robert Johnston, "Terrorist Attacks in Russia," January 26, 2011, http://www.johnstonsarchive.net/terrorism/terr-russia.html.
3. Anders Aslund, Sergei Guriev, and Andrew C. Kuchins, eds., *Russia After the Global Economic Crisis* (Washington, DC: Peterson Institute for International Economy: Center for Strategic and International Policy; Moscow: New Economic School, June 2010), 26; Trading Economics, *Saudi Arabia GDP Growth Rate*, http://www.tradingeconomics.com/Economics/GDP-Growth.
4. Aslund, Guriev, and Kuchins, eds., *Russia After the Economic Crisis,* 12.
5. Thomas Remington, *Politics in Russia*, 7th ed. (Boston: Longman, 2012), 210.
6. Michael Schwirtz, "Putin Marks Soviet Massacre of Polish Officers," *New York Times*, April 8, 2010.
7. In late September 2009, the European Union published the *Report of the Independent International Fact-Finding Mission on the Conflict in Georgia*, which supports the interpretation advanced in this book. For the text of the report, see http://www.ceiig.ch/.

Chapter 1. The Formative Years (1952–1990)

1. Roy Medvedev, *Vladimir Putin: Chetyre goda v Kremle* [Vladimir Putin: Four Years in the Kremlin] (Moscow: Vremya, 2004), 252.
2. The city was called St. Petersburg between 1703 and 1914, Petrograd in 1914–1924, Leningrad in 1924–1991, and again St. Petersburg since 1991.
3. Oleg Blotskiy, *Vladimir Putin: Istoriya zhizni* [Vladimir Putin: The story of his life] (Moscow: Mezhdunarodnye Otnosheniya, 2002), 37–38.

4. Nikolai Zen'kovich, ed., *Putinskaya entsiklopediya* [The Putin encyclopedia] (Moscow: OLMA Media Grupp, 2008), 401–2; Vladimir Putin, *First Person: An Astonishingly Frank Self-Portrait by Russia's President*, trans. Catherine Fitzpatrick (New York: Public Affairs, 2000), 3; and Blotskiy, *Vladimir Putin: Istoriya zhizni*, 38.

5. This family experience should be kept in mind when evaluating Putin's reactions in the spring of 2007 to the Estonian government's relocation of a Soviet war memorial from downtown Tallinn to the city's outskirts. Afterward a barrage of sophisticated hacking operations of Russian provenance suddenly and mysteriously overwhelmed Estonian government computer systems. The Russians' crude but widespread postwar belief that the Baltic peoples were "fascistic," given that many in the countries—recently annexed and savagely repressed by Stalin—welcomed the Nazis as liberators, finds specific personal resonance in Putin's immediate family history.

6. Blotskiy, *Vladimir Putin: Istoriya zhizni*, 38, 79 passim.

7. Zen'kovich, *Putinskaya entsiklopediya*, 396–99; Putin, *First Person*, 3–4; and Oleg Blotskiy, *Vladimir Putin: Doroga k vlasti* [Vladimir Putin: The road to power] (Moscow: Osmos Press, 2002), 256.

8. Zen'kovich, *Putinskaya entsiklopediya*, 411–13; and Leonid Mlechin, *Kreml': Prezidenty Rossii: Strategiya vlasti ot B. N. El'tsina do V. V. Putina* [The Kremlin: Presidents of Russia: The strategy of power from Yeltsin to Putin] (Moscow: Tsentrpoligraf, 2003), 26.

9. Alexander Rahr claims that she was executed by the Nazis as a partisan, or as a Soviet guerrilla fighter. See Alexander Rahr, *Putin nach Putin: Das kapitalistische Russland am Beginn einer neuen Weltordunung* (Munich: Universitas-Verlag, 2008), 41. Putin himself has stated that it was never clear whether his grandmother died from Nazi or Soviet shrapnel in a hail of artillery fire. Zen'kovich, *Putinskaya entsiklopediya*, 571.

10. Blotskiy, *Vladimir Putin: Istoriya zhizni*, 25.

11. Tom Streissguth, *Vladimir Putin* (Minneapolis: Lerner Publications, 2005), 11.

12. Charles J. Shields, *Vladimir Putin* (New York: Chelsea House Publishers, 2007), 32.

13. Putin, *First Person*, 6.

14. Blotskiy, *Vladimir Putin: Istoriya zhizni*, 26.

15. Putin, *First Person*, 11–12, 21.

16. Elena Krivyakina, "Putin Presented Former Teacher Apartment," *Komsomol'skaya Pravda*, October 4, 2007, http://www.kp.ru/daily/23979.3/74288/print/.

17. Nina Tumarkin, *The Living and the Dead: The Rise and Fall of the Cult of World War II in Russia* (New York: Basic Books, 1994).

18. Blotskiy, *Vladimir Putin: Istoriya zhizni*, 211.

19. Mlechin, *Kreml'*, 28; and Pierre Lorrain, *La mystérieuse ascension du Vladimir Poutine* (Paris: Editions du Rocher, 2002), 107.

20. Blotskiy, *Vladimir Putin: Istoriya zhizni*, 59–62.

21. Sambo is a Russian acronym meaning "self-defense without weapons."

22. Lorrain, *Mystérieuse ascension*, 93–94, 129, 447; and Putin, *First Person*, 18–23, 92.

23. Mlechin, *Kreml'*, 29; and Blotskiy, *Vladimir Putin: Istoriya zhizni*, 218.

24. Medvedev, *Vladimir Putin: Chetyre goda v Kremle*, 10, 17.

25. Putin, *First Person*, 32–33; and Zen'kovich, *Putinskaya entsiklopediya*, 7, 302.

26. Tony Halpin, "Vladimir Putin Flies in Bjorn Again for Abba Tribute Concert," *The Times (London)*, February 6, 2009, http://www.timesonline.co.uk/tol/news /world/europe/article5671675.ece.

27. Putin, *First Person*, 38–39.

28. Streissguth, *Vladimir Putin*, 21; Blotskiy, *Vladimir Putin: Istoriya zhizni*, 308; and Putin, *First Person*, 41.

29. Boris Reitschuster, *Putins Demokratur: Wie der Kreml den Westen das Fuerchten lehrt* (Berlin: Ullstein, 2006), 65; and Mlechin, *Kreml'*, 31, 34.

30. Zen'kovich, *Putinskaya entsiklopediya*, 54, 57–58, 405.

31. Konrad Rufus Müller and Katja Gloger, *Wladimir Putin* (Goettingen, Germany: Steidl Gerhard Verlag, 2003), 21–22, 51–52, 62.

32. Blotskiy, *Vladimir Putin: Doroga k vlasti*, 50–51.

33. Müller and Gloger, *Wladimir Putin*, 21–22, 51–52, 62.

34. Putin, *First Person*, 53, 60. Details about the maneuvering behind Putin's nomination to Dresden are included in Blotskiy, *Vladimir Putin: Doroga k vlasti*, 209–12.

35. Putin, *First Person*, 70–71, 75, 77; and Blotskiy, *Vladimir Putin: Doroga k vlasti*, 219, 252–53.

36. Zen'kovich, *Putinskaya entsiklopediya*, 45, 103; Lorrain, *Mystérieuse ascension*, 160, 167; and Mlechin, *Kreml'*, 40.

37. For a recording of Putin's recollection of the events, see Blotskiy, *Vladimir Putin: Doroga k vlasti*, 259–61.

38. As cited in Reitschuster, *Putins Demokratur*, 28.

39. Boris Reitschuster, *Wladimir Putin: Wohin steuert er Russland?* (Berlin: Rowohlt, 2004), 23.

40. Blotskiy, *Vladimir Putin: Doroga k vlasti*, 265.

41. Reitschuster, *Wladimir Putin*, 25.

42. Reitschuster, *Putins Demokratur*, 24, 28; and Rahr, *Putin nach Putin*, 70.

Chapter 2. In St. Petersburg's City Hall (1990–1996)

1. Zen'kovich, *Putinskaya entsiklopediya*, 611.

2. Blotskiy, *Vladimir Putin: Doroga k vlasti*, 280–87.

3. Lorrain, *Mystérieuse ascension*, 240; and Putin, *First Person*, 86.

4. Mlechin, *Kreml'*, 46.

5. Streissguth, *Vladimir Putin*, 39.

6. Zen'kovich, *Putinskaya entsiklopediya*, 462.

7. Lorrain, *Mystérieuse ascension*, 241–42.

8. See Blotskiy, *Vladimir Putin: Doroga k vlasti*, 367; and Putin, *First Person*, 97–102.

9. Medvedev, *Vladimir Putin*, 23, 39–40; Rahr, *Putin nach Putin*, 89; and Anatoly Sobchak, *Dyuzhina nozhei v spinu* [A dozen knives in the back] (Moscow: Vagrius, 1999), 70–71.

10. Sobchak, *Dyuzhina nozhei*, 35–36.

11. Lorrain, *Mystérieuse ascension*, 242–43.

12. Rahr, *Putin nach Putin*, 79.

13. Müeller and Gloger, *Wladimir Putin,* 82.

14. Zen'kovich, *Putinskaya entsiklopediya,* 464.

15. Ibid., 299.

16. As recounted in Medvedev, *Vladimir Putin,* 32.

17. Ibid., 44–46.

18. As it turned out, Sobchak's heart condition was so serious that the doctors in Paris refused to operate on him. He was advised to take an extensive rest and retire from politics. Sobchak refused to follow their advice, no doubt contributing to his untimely demise in February 2000.

19. Ibid., 53–55. Sobchak confirms all of the essentials of the dramatic flight although, writing in July 1999, he tactfully does not mention Putin's role in a manifestly "illegal" operation. See Sobchak, *Dyuzhina nozhei,* 145–67.

20. Boris Yeltsin, *Prezidentskiy marafon* [Presidential marathon] (Moscow: AST, 2000), 360; and Medvedev, *Vladimir Putin,* 63.

21. Blotskiy, *Vladimir Putin: Doroga k vlasti,* 374.

22. "Researchers Peg Putin as a Plagiarist over Thesis," *Washington Times,* March 24, 2006; and Vladimir Vladimirovich Putin, "Strategic Planning for Rehabilitation of the Mineral Resources Base of the Region during the Formation of Market Relations," in *The Uppsala Yearbook of East European Law,* ed. and trans. Kaj Hobér (London: Wildy, Simmonds & Hill Publishing, 2006), 301–478. Putin approved the translation himself before the charges of plagiarism were launched against him. For evidence of plagiarism, compare the charts in Putin, "Strategic Planning," 348, 354, and 357, with those in William King and David Cleland, *Strategic Planning and Policy* (New York: Van Nostrand Reinhold, 1978), 22, 91, and 33, respectively; and in Putin, "Strategic Planning," 346 and 353, with King and Cleland, *Strategic Planning,* 20 and 91, respectively. See also Putin, "Strategic Planning," 413–30, for improbable evidence of Putin's mathematical acumen. A summary translation of Putin's thesis is also available: V. V. Putin, "Mineral and Raw Materials Resources and the Development Strategy for the Russian Economy" (doctorate thesis, Saint Petersburg, 1999), trans. Thomas Fennell, 2008, www.docstoc.com/docs/1064312/Putins-Thesis.

23. Alain Guillemoles and Alla Lazareva, *Gazprom: Le nouvel empire* (Paris: Les Petits Matins, 2008), 109.

24. For discussion in detail, see Harley Balzer, "The Putin Thesis and Russian Energy Policy," *Post-Soviet Affairs* 21, no. 3 (2005): 210–25; and Ulrich G. Klaus and Thomas Waelde, "The Role of State Control over Natural Resources and the Economy in Russia: Some Salient Issues in President Putin's Academic Writing," in Hobér, *The Uppsala Yearbook,* 267–92.

25. Putin, "Mineral and Raw Materials Resources."

26. Klaus and Waelde, "Role of State Control," 290.

Chapter 3. To Moscow and the Top (1996–1999)

1. As cited by Boris Mazo, *Preemnik Putina, ili Kogo my budem vybirat' v 2008 godu* [Putin's successor, or whom are we going to vote for in 2008?] (Moscow: Algorithm, 2005), 17.

2. Allen C. Lynch, *How Russia Is Not Ruled: Reflections on Russian Political Development* (New York: Cambridge University Press, 2005).

3. William Zimmerman, *The Russian People and Foreign Policy: Russian Elite and Mass Perspectives, 1993–2000* (Princeton, NJ: Princeton University Press, 2002).

4. Anders Aslund, "Social Problems and Policy in Postcommunist Russia," in *Sustaining the Transition: The Social Safety Net in Postcommunist Europe,* ed. Ethan B. Kapstein and Michael Mandelbaum (New York: Council on Foreign Relations, 1997), 125–28.

5. A. D. Andrianov, *Rossiya v mirovoy ekonomike* [Russia in the World Economy] (Moscow: Vlados, 1999), 22.

6. The Russian *privatizatsiya* (privatization) was turned into *prikhvatizatsiya,* which translates easily as "piratization." See Marshall Goldman, *The Piratization of Russia: Russian Reform Goes Awry* (London: Routledge, 2003).

7. *Liberation* (Paris), "Le directeur général du Fonds monétaire international: 'La Russie a mis un coup de canif dans son contrat avec le FMI'" [IMF director: "Russia put a penknife blow in his contract with the IMF"]. August 31, 1999, http://www.liberation.fr/evenement/0101289479-le-directeur-general-du-fonds -monetaire-international-la-russie-a-mis-un-coup-de-canif-dans-son-contrat -avec-le-fmi-dans-une-interview-a-liberation-michel-camdessus-s-exprime-sur- les-accusations-de-de.

8. Allen Lynch, "Russia: Report Card on Survival," in *Great Decisions 2000,* ed. Foreign Policy Association (New York: Foreign Policy Association, 2000), 22–28.

9. Medvedev, *Vladimir Putin,* 82.

10. Ibid., 95–96.

11. Blotskiy, *Vladimir Putin: Doroga k vlasti,* quoting Putin extensively, 383–94; Medvedev, *Vladimir Putin,* 47; and Lorrain, *Mystérieuse ascension,* 378–79.

12. Michael Stuermer, *Putin and the Rise of Russia* (London: Weidenfeld & Nicholson, 2008), 25.

13. Mlechin, *Kreml',* 565.

14. Reitschuster, *Wladimir Putin,* 46.

15. Ibid., 41–42, 46.

16. Rahr, *Putin nach Putin,* 119.

17. Reitschuster, *Wladimir Putin,* 48–51.

18. Vladimir Solovyov and Nikolay Zlobin, *Putin-Medvedev: Chto dal'she?* [Putin-Medvedev: What Next?] (Moscow: Eksmo, 2010), 40–43.

19. Yeltsin, *Prezidentskiy marafon,* 315, 354–64, and especially 358–59.

20. As related in Medvedev, *Vladimir Putin,* 64–66.

21. Zen'kovich, *Putinskaya entsiklopediya,* 7.

Chapter 4. Putin At the Helm (1999–2000)

1. As cited in Thierry Wolton, *Le KGB au pouvoir: Le système Poutine* (Paris: Buchet/ Chastel, 2008), 119.

2. See Medvedev, *Vladimir Putin,* 100–137, for a detailed and balanced account of the Chechnyan conflict during Putin's accession to power.

3. Yeltsin, *Prezidentskiy marafon,* 386–87; and Zen'kovich, *Putinskaya entsiklopediya,* 6–7.

4. Medvedev, *Vladimir Putin*, 101.

5. Lorrain, *Mystérieuse ascension*, 429–30. Lorrain bases this account on personal conversations with Sergei Stepashin, who was prime minister when the plan was developed in the spring of 1999.

6. Johnston, "Terrorist Attacks in Russia."

7. As cited in Lorrain, *Mystérieuse ascension*, 441.

8. Medvedev, *Vladimir Putin*, 103.

9. Daniel Treisman, "Presidential Popularity in a Hybrid Regime: Russia Under Yeltsin and Putin," *American Journal of Political Science*, February 1, 2011, http://www.sscnet.ucla.edu/polisci/faculty/treisman/PAPERS_NEW/Pres%20pop%20final%20for%20website.pdf.

10. The charges focus on the consequences of the announcement on September 22, 2009, by city authorities in Ryazan, south of Moscow, that a neighborhood vigilante committee had foiled a terrorist plot to blow up a fifth apartment building. Putin publicly announced that another terrorist plot had been foiled. It then turned out that the individuals arrested in the basement of a Ryazan apartment building with sacks of white powder initially identified as the military explosive RDX were in fact FSB agents. FSB officials then explained that the substance was in fact sugar and that the agents had been involved in a training exercise designed to test citizens' vigilance. Without further clarification by the government, many questioned the government's possible role in the September bombings. See Reitschuster, *Putins Demokratur*, 35–36.

11. Lorrain, *Mystérieuse ascension*, 440.

12. As cited in ibid., 431.

13. As recounted and cited in ibid., 431.

14. Mlechin, *Kreml'*, 579. This is the judgment of Mlechin, a frequent Putin critic.

15 Yeltsin, *Prezidentskiy marafon*, 368.

16. By contrast, back in the summer of 1996, Boris Yeltsin suffered a heart attack between the first and second rounds of the presidential elections. Berezovsky and his allies in the Russian media managed to keep the news a secret until after the second round had been completed and Yeltsin had emerged victorious. They also kept secret the extensive involvement of U.S. election strategists, sent by the White House, to help manage Yeltsin's reelection.

17. As cited in Richard Rose and Neil Munro, *Elections without Order: Russia's Challenge to Vladimir Putin* (Cambridge: Cambridge University Press, 2002), 165.

18. Ibid.

19. An English translation of Putin's article may be found in Richard Sakwa, *Putin: Russia's Choice*, 2nd ed. (London: Routledge, 2007), 317–28.

20. Vladimir V. Putin, *Izbrannye rechi i vystupleniya* [Selected speeches and addresses] (Moscow: Knizhnyi mir, 2008), 6.

21. Yeltsin, *Prezidentskiy marafon*, 13–14; and Medvedev, *Vladimir Putin*, 77–79.

22. The fiercely anti-Putin journalist Yevgeniya Albats described Putin as a mirror reflecting the mood of Russian society. As cited in Zen'kovich, *Putinskaya entsiklopediya*, 28.

23. For relevant Russian public opinion polling, see the website of the independent Levada center, http://www.levada.ru/prez07.html and in English at http://www.russiavotes.org/.

24. Rose and Munro, *Elections without Order*, 169, 177.

Chapter 5. Putin in Power: Domestic Politics and Policies

1. As cited in Wolton, *Le KGB au pouvoir*, 157.

2. Putin, *Izbrannye rechi i vystupleniya*, 77–79.

3. Roy Medvedev, *Vladimir Putin: Vtoroy srok* [Vladimir Putin: The second term] (Moscow: Vremya, 2006), 14.

4. Putin, *Izbrannye rechi i vystupleniya*, 5–6.

5. Medvedev, *Vladimir Putin: Vtoroy srok*, 14–15.

6. Olga Kryshtanovskaya, "Authoritarian Modernization of Russia in the 2000s," in *What Does Russia Think?*, eds. Ivan Krastev, Mark Leonard, and Andrew Wilson (London: European Council on Foreign Relations, 2009), 28–32.

7. "The State of Russia," *The Economist*, December 9, 2010.

8. Vladimir Solovyov, *Putin: Putevoditel' dlya neravnodushnykh* [Putin: A Guide for those who cannot stay indifferent] (Moscow: Eksmo, 2008).

9. Olga Kryshtanovskaya, *Anatomiya rossiyskoy elity* [Anatomy of the Russian elite] (Moscow: Zakharov, 2005); and Medvedev, *Vladimir Putin: Vtoroy srok*, 43.

10. Stephen K. Wegren, "Agriculture in the Late Putin Period and Beyond," in *After Putin's Russia: Past Imperfect, Future Uncertain*, 4th ed., eds., Stephen K. Wegren and Dale R. Herspring (Lanham, MD: Rowman & Littlefield, 2010), 199–220.

11. Christine Ebrahim-zadeh, "Dutch Disease: Too much wealth managed unwisely," *Finance and Development Online*; "Back to Basics," March 2003, http://www.imf.org/external/pubs/ft/fandd/2003/03/ebra.htm.

12. Aslund, Guriev, and Kuchins, eds., *Russia After the Economic Crisis*, 1.

13. Kevin O'Flynn, "Creaking Infrastructure Evident from Siberia to the Streets of Moscow," Radio Free Europe/Radio Liberty, as cited in *Johnson's Russia List* no. 170 (September 12, 2009), item 24, www.cdi.org/russia/johnson/2009-170-24.cfm.

14. Aslund, Guriev, and Kuchins, eds., *Russia After the Economic Crisis*, 16.

15. Transparency International, "Corruptions Perception Index 2010 Results," October 26, 2010, http://www.transparency.org/policy_research/surveys_indices/cpi/2010/results.

16. Sergey N. Bobylev et al., *National Human Development Report in the Russian Federation, 2009: Energy Sector and Sustainable Development*. Moscow: United Nations Development Program, 2010; Maria Antonova, "Risk of 'Dutch Disease' Worsening by 2020, UN Says," *Moscow Times*, April 20, 2010.

17. On the concept of Putin's Russia as a "kleptocracy," see Emma M. Whyte, PhD candidate, "Government Profit-Seeking and Policy Outcomes in Russia's Petrostate," (unpublished paper, Woodrow Wilson Department of Politics, University of Virginia, Charlottesville, VA, January 2011).

18. Mlechin, *Kreml'*, 645.

19. Solovyov, *Putin*, 130.

20. Lorrain, *Mystérieuse ascension*, 444–45.

21. Lilia Shevtsova, *Russia, Lost in Transition: The Yeltsin and Putin Legacies*, trans. Arch Tait (Washington, DC: Carnegie Endowment for International Peace, 2007), 48, 50, 70–71.

22. Olivier Ravanello, *L'oeil de Moscou* (Paris: Les editions du Toucan, 2008), 91.

23. The substance of the report is discussed later in this chapter (see "Boundaries of Power") and in the conclusion of this volume.

24. Committee to Protect Journalists, "Yuri Shchekochikhin: Novaya Gazeta," http://www.cpj.org/killed/2003/yuri-shchekochikhin.php.

25. Obituary, "Anna Politkovskaya, a Russian journalist, was shot dead on October 7th, aged 48," *The Economist*, October 12, 2006, http://www.economist.com node/8023316.

26. Reitschuster, *Putins Demokratur*, 93–94.

27. Arkadi Vaksberg, *Le laboratoire des poisons: De Lénine à Poutine*, trans. Luba Jurgenson (Paris: Editions Gallimard, 2008), 355–57.

28. Andrei Illarionov, "*Silovaya model' gosudarstva: predvaritel'nye itogi*" [The "power model" of the state: preliminary results], *Kommersant*, April 2, 2007, 2. For a compatible interpretation of the media's fate under Putin, see Maria Lipman and Michael McFaul, "The Media and Political Developments," in Wegren and Herspring, *After Putin's Russia*, 109–29.

29. Freedom House, "Russia 2010," *Freedom of the Press 2010: Broad Setbacks to Global Media Freedom*, http://www.freedomhouse.org/uploads/fop10/Global_Table_2010.pdf.

30. Andrew Wilson, *Virtual Politics: Faking Democracy in the Post-Soviet World* (New Haven, CT: Yale University Press, 2005).

31. Portions of what follows on Putin's "machine" have been revised and updated from the author's "Russia and 'Putinism,'" in *Great Decisions 2008*, ed. Foreign Policy Association (New York: Foreign Policy Association, 2008), 43–48. For a thoughtful if somewhat idealized Russian interpretation of Putinism, see Andranik Migranyan, "What Is 'Putinism'?," *Russia in Global Affairs* 17, no. 2 (April 13, 2004): 25, www.eng.globalaffairs.ru/number/n_2902.

32. See Alexander J. Motyl, Blair A. Ruble, and Lilia Shevtsova, eds., *Russia's Engagement with the West: Transformation and Integration in the Twenty-First Century* (Armonk, NY: M. E. Sharpe, 2005), 8–9, 99–120; Luke March, "Managing Opposition in a Hybrid Regime: Just Russia and Parastatal Opposition," *Slavic Review* 68, no. 3 (Fall 2009): 504–27; and Graeme B. Robertson, "Managed Society: Protest, Civil Society, and Regime in Putin's Russia," *Slavic Review* 68, no. 3 (Fall 2009): 528–47.

33. Raymond E. Wolfinger, "Why Political Machines Have Not Withered Away and Other Revisionist Thoughts," *Journal of Politics* 34, no. 2 (1972): 365–98; Jacob M. Schlesinger, *Shadow Shoguns: The Rise and Fall of Japan's Postwar Political Machine* (Palo Alto: Stanford University Press, 1999); Judith Chubb, "The Social Bases of an Urban Political Machine: The Case of Palermo," *Political Science Quarterly* 96, no. 1 (1981): 101–125; V. O. Key, *Southern Politics in State and Nation* (New York: Alfred Knopf, 1949).

34. Remington, *Politics in Russia*, 208.

35. Kathryn Hendley, "The Law in Post-Putin Russia," in Wegren and Herspring, *After Putin's Russia*, 83–108.

36. For a comprehensive and authoritative account of the Khodorkovsky affair, see Richard Sakwa, *The Quality of Freedom: Khodorkovsky, Putin, and the Yukos Affair* (Oxford, UK: Oxford University Press, 2009).

37. For examples, see Zen'kovich, *Putinskaya entsiklopediya*, 535–37.

38. As cited in Wolton, *Le KGB au pouvoir*, 185.

39. Margareta Mommsen and Angelika Nussberger, *Das System Putin: Gelenkte Demokratie und politische Justiz in Russland* (Munich: C. H. Beck, 2007), 140.

40. RIA Novosti, "Putin on Khodorkovsky: 'A Thief Belongs Behind Bars,'" December 16, 2010, www.en.rian.ru/russia/20101216/161802103.html.

41. Robert W. Orttung, "Russia," *Nations in Transit, 2010* (Washington, DC: Freedom House, 2010), 447, http://www.freedomhouse.eu/images/Reports/NIT-2010-Russia-final.pdf.

42. Reitschuster, *Putins Demokratur*, 55–64. Reitschuster, a German journalist covering Kasparov, was an eyewitness to many of these incidents.

43. Rafael Guseinov, "Orientiry Prezidenta" [The President's Orientation], *Trud*, July 20, 2001.

44. Thomas F. Remington, *Politics in Russia*, 6th ed. (Boston: Longman, 2010), 9.

45. Rajan Menon and Alexander J. Motyl, "The Myth of Russian Resurgence," *The American Interest Online*, March–April 2007.

46. Boris Nemtsov and Vladimir Milov, *Nezavisimyi ekspertnyi doklad: Putin, Itogi* [An Independent Experts' Report: Putin, the Results] (Moscow: Novaya Gazeta, 2008), 9; Reitschuster, *Putins Demokratur*, 116–17.

47. Reitschuster, *Putins Demokratur*, 179. For corresponding U.S. and Spanish government assessments of the extent of criminalization among Russian political elites, see materials made available by Wikileaks, "2011-02-25 Russia and Spain: Organized Crime, Half-Truths and Public Secrets," http://wicentral.org/node/1372, and Luke Harding, "Wikileaks Cables Condemn Russia as 'Mafia State,'" Guardian.co.uk, December 1, 2010, http://www.guardian.co.uk/world/2010/dec/01/wikileaks-cables-russia-mafia-kleptocracy.

48. See Zen'kovich, *Putinskaya entsiklopediya*, 251; and Reitschuster, *Putins Demokratur*, 155.

49. Nemtsov and Milov, *Nezavisimyi ekspertnyi doklad*, 10–11.

50. Ibid., 12–13.

51. The World Bank and the International Finance Corporation, *Doing Business 2011* (Washington, DC: The World Bank, 2010), 4, 26, http://www.doingbusiness.org/~/media/FPDKM/Doing%20Business/Documents/Annual-Reports/English/DB11-FullReport.pdf.

52. Not surprisingly, Russia has the lowest ratio of foreign direct investment to GDP of any leading emerging-market economy, and just one-third that of China. Transparency International, *Corruption Perceptions Index 2010*, http://www.transparency.org/policy-research/surveys_indices/cpi/2010.results; "Russia's Dismal Investment Climate," *The Economist*, July 2, 2009, http://www.economist.com/node/13962526; Henry Meyer, "Russia Repels Retailers as Ikea Halt

Curtails Medvedev Goals," *Bloomberg,* March 2, 2011, http://www.bloomberg .com/news/2011-03-01/russia-repels-retailers-as-ikea-halt-curtails-medvedev -bric-goal.html.

53. "Uroven' odobreniya deyatel'nosti V. Putina na postu prezidenta Rossii [Level of Approval of Vladimir Putin's performance as President of Russia], July 11, 2011, http://www.levada.ru/prezident.html and http://www.russia votes.org/.

54. See Allen C. Lynch, "The Putin Succession and Russian Foreign Policy," *The Brown Journal of World Affairs* 14, no. 1 (Fall/Winter 2007): 53–64.

55. As cited in Melissa Payne, "Putin: The Sun that Never Sets?," *World Politics Review,* March 27, 2007, http://www.worldpoliticsreview.com/article.aspx?id=658.

56. Michael L. Bressler, "Politics," in *Understanding Contemporary Russia,* ed. Michael L. Bressler (Boulder, CO: Lynne Rienner, 2009), 124–25.

57. For examples of these ads, see http://www.medvedev2008.ru/avm.htm.

58. As cited in Zen'kovich, *Putinskaya entsiklopediya,* 28. See also Reitschuster, *Putins Demokratur,* 321.

59. For supporting evidence and argumentation, see Ellen Carnaghan, *Out of Order: Russian Political Values in an Imperfect World* (University Park: Pennsylvania State University Press, 2007), 73–105.

Chapter 6. Putin in Power: Foreign Policy

1. As cited in Wolton, *Le KGB au pouvoir,* 199.

2. In a strategy statement approved by the Russian National Security Council on May 12, 2009, Russia's security challenges are defined as overwhelmingly internal in character, while the substantive external challenges relate mainly to the United States, the European Union, and the post-Soviet region. China is mentioned in passing twice and the Asian-Pacific region not at all. "Strategiya natsional'noy bezopasnosti Rossiyskoy Federatsii do 2020 goda" [Russian national security strategy up to 2020], no. 537, March 12, 2009, http://www.scrf. gov.ru/documents/99.html.

3. J. L. Black, *Vladimir Putin and the New World Order: Looking East, Looking West?* (Lanham, MD: Rowman & Littlefield, 2003), 107; and Reitschuster, *Putins Demokratur,* 238–39.

4. Alex Pravda, "Putin's Foreign Policy after 11 September: Radical or Revolutionary?," in *Russia between East and West: Russian Foreign Policy on the Threshold of the Twenty-First Century,* ed. G. Gorodetsky (London: Cass, 2003), 39–57; and Andrei Tsygankov, "Vladimir Putin's Vision of Russia as a Normal Great Power," *Post-Soviet Affairs* 21, no. 2 (April–June 2005).

5. James Goldgeier and Michael McFaul, *Power and Purpose: U.S. Policy Toward Russia after the Cold War* (Washington, DC: Brookings, 2003), 297–99.

6. Putin, *Izbrannye rechi i vystupleniya,* 77–79.

7. Goldgeier and McFaul, *Power and Purpose,* 273, 276–78, 310.

8. Black, *Vladimir Putin,* 42; and Mommsen and Nussberger, *Das System Putin,* 164.

9. Goldgeier and McFaul, *Power and Purpose,* 275; and Mommsen and Nussberger, *Das System Putin,* 164.

10. Reitschuster, *Wladimir Putin*, 12.

11. Pierre Lorrain, *L'Incroyable alliance Russie–Etas-Unis* (Paris: Editions du Rocher, 2002), 9–39; and Goldgeier and McFaul, *Power and Purpose*, 313–20.

12. As cited in Thomas Ambrosio, "The Russo-American Dispute over the Invasion of Iraq: International Status and the Role of Positional Goods," *Europe-Asia Studies* 57, no. 8 (December 2005): 1195.

13. Black, *Vladimir Putin*, 160–61.

14. Patrick E. Tyler, "A Nation Challenged: The Caucasus; Russia's Leader Says He Supports American Military Aid for Georgia," *New York Times*, March 2, 2002.

15. Zen'kovich, *Putinskaya entsiklopediya*, 441.

16. Greg White, "Gorby's Choice," *Wall Street Journal*, December 1, 2007. See also Jack F. Matlock, Jr., *Superpower Illusions: How Myths and False Ideologies Led America Astray—and How to Return to Reality* (New Haven, CT: Yale University Press, 2010).

17. Black, *Vladimir Putin*, 161, 174.

18. Medvedev, *Vladimir Putin: Chetrye goda v Kremlye*, 397–402. For the English text of Putin's speech, see, "Putin Addresses German Parliament in Russian and then German," BBC Monitoring Service (United Kingdom, September 25, 2001), www.cdi.org/russia/johnson/5460.html#%232.

19. Alexander Rahr, *Russland gibt Gas: Die Rueckkehr einer Weltmacht* (Munich: Carl Hanser Wirtschaftg, 2008), 209.

20. For insights into French calculations, see Reneo Lukic, ed., *Conflit et coopération dans les relations Franco-Américaines* (Quebec: Les Presses de l'Université Laval, 2009), 183–212, 250–57, 317–19.

21. The ensuing discussion draws from Ambrosio, "Russo-American Dispute," 1196–1204.

22. "Interview Granted by President Vladimir Putin to France-3 Television," *Official Kremlin International News Broadcast*, February 10, 2003, as cited in Ambrosio, "Russo-American Dispute," 1202.

23. Medvedev, *Vladimir Putin: Chetyre goda v Kremle*, 556–57.

24. As cited in Ambrosio, "Russo-American Dispute," 1204.

25. "After Russian Invasion of Georgia, Putin's Words Stir Fears About Ukraine," *Kyiv Post*, November 30, 2010.

26. Rahr, *Russland gibt Gas*, 112.

27. Pavel K. Baev, *Russian Energy Policy and Military Power: Putin's Quest for Greatness* (London: Routledge, 2008), 150; and Reitschuster, *Putins Demokratur*, 19.

28. Zen'kovich, *Putinskaya entsiklopediya*, 616.

29. Ibid., 603.

30. Personal communication from Gustav Weber, a German election observer in Ukraine in the fall of 2004 working under the auspices of the Organization for Security and Cooperation in Europe.

31. Andrew Wilson, *Ukraine's Orange Revolution* (New Haven, CT: Yale University Press, 2005), 96–99; Vaksberg, *Le laboratoire des poisons*, 337–42; and Elisabeth Rosenthal, "American Doctors Helped Identify Ukraine Leader's Poisoning," *International Herald Tribune*, March 13, 2005.

32. Yushchenko also had a catheter inserted with a powerful painkiller fed intravenously into his body.

33. Baev, *Russian Energy Policy*, 124.

34. Adrian Karatnycky and Alexander J. Motyl, "The Key to Kiev: Ukraine's Security Means Europe's Stability," *Foreign Affairs*, May/June 2009, 106.

35. Eighty percent of Russia's natural gas deliveries to Europe flow through pipelines transecting Ukraine.

36. Ellen Barry, "Russia's Neighbors Resist Wooing and Bullying," *New York Times*, July 3, 2009.

37. Peter Baker, "Obama Resets Ties to Russia, but Work Remains," *New York Times*, July 7, 2009.

Conclusion: To 2012 and Beyond

1. Journalists overheard Vladislav Surkov briefing members of parliament. See Mlechin, *Kreml'*, 679.

2. Mikhail Dertagin, "Tyuning 'sovka'" [A Tuning Fork], *Novaya Gazeta*, August 21, 2009, www.novayagazeta.ru/data/091/01.html.

3. James R. Millar, "The Economy," in Bressler, *Understanding Contemporary Russia*, 153.

4. U.S. Department of State, "Background Note: Russia," March 16, 2011, http://www.state.gov/r/pa/ei/bgn/3183.htm.

5. Remington, *Politics in Russia* (7th ed., 2012), 209.

6. Gregory L. White, "S&P Downgrades Russia, Citing Falling Reserves," *Wall Street Journal*, December 9, 2008.

7. "Background Note: Russia."

8. Andrew E. Kramer, "Russia Gains at OPEC's Expense," *New York Times*, October 19, 2009.

9. Remington, *Politics in Russia*, 216.

10. Ibid., 210.

11. Ibid., 193.

12. *Wall Street Journal* online, "Putin Speaks at Davos," January 28, 2009, http://online.wsj.com/article/SB123317069332125243.html.

13. Nemtsov and Milov, *Nezavisimyi ekspertnyi doklad*, 76. Five thousand copies of the report were published, and it is freely available on the Internet, including in Russia itself. See the extensive review of the report by Amy Knight, "The Truth about Putin and Medvedev," *New York Review of Books*, May 15, 2008, www.nybooks.com/articles/archives/2008/may/15/the-truth-about-putin-and-medvedev/. For President Medvedev's analysis, see Dmitri Medvedev, "Go, Russia!," September 10, 2009, http://eng.kremlin.ru/news/298.

14. Nemtsov and Milov, *Nezavisimyi ekspertnyi doklad*, 61.

15. See Solovyov's otherwise favorable account of Putin's presidency, *Putin*, 415–16.

16. Apart from Milov and Nemtsov, see Dmitri Dokuchaev and Dmitri Krylov, "Dorogi, Kotorye nas Obirayut" [The Roads that Rob Us], *Novoye Vremya*, no. 8, March 8, 2010; see also Aleksey Tarasov, "Edinaya Rossiya ot Kaliningrada do Chiti" [A United Russia from Kaliningrad to Chita], *Novaya Gazeta*, April 5, 2010.

17. Paul Goble, "Window on Eurasia: Corruption Keeping Russian Highways among Worst in World, Investigators Say," *Johnson's Russia List*, no. 46, March 8, 2010, item 5, www.cdi.org/russia/johnson.

18. Vladislav Inozemtsev, "Dilemmas of Russia's Modernization," in Krastev, Leonard, and Wilson, *What Does Russia Think?*, 50. The same is true of metals processing plants.

19. Joe Nocera, "Guilty Verdict for a Tycoon, and Russia," *New York Times*, December 31, 2010.

20. ING, "Russian Oil Majors Ask for Help," October 2008. I am grateful to Hugh Ragsdale for having brought this report to my attention. For details on the impact of economic geography on Russian costs of production and on recent Russian drilling practices, see Lynch, *How Russia Is Not Ruled*, chapter 6; and Guillemoles and Lazareva, *Gazprom*, 156.

21. Russian infrastructure investment between 1990 and 2007 as a percentage of GDP stands at 2.3 percent, or half of the level in the United States and Canada (4.6 percent) and well below the global average (4.2 percent) and that for post-communist Eastern Europe (5.3 percent). Liam Denning, "Russia's Infrastructure Plan a Risky Play," *Wall Street Journal*, January 5, 2009.

22. Aslund, Guriev, and Kuchins, eds., *Russia After the Economic Crisis*, 153.

23. BBC Mobile, "Putin Aide Sobyanin Confirmed as Moscow Mayor," *BBC*, October 21, 2010, http://www.bbc.co.uk/news/world-europe-11596511.

24. Solovyov and Zlobin, *Putin-Medvedev*, 112–14.

25. Solovyov, *Putin*, 416.

26. Ibid.

27. Ibid.

28. Mazo, *Preemnik Putina*, 6.

29. "Uroven' odobreniya deyatel'nosti V. Putina na postu predsedatelya pravitel'stva [Level of Approval of Vladimir Putin's performance as Prime Minister], July 11, 2011, www.levada.ru/premyer.html.

30. Economist Intelligence Unit, *Democracy Index 2010* (London: EIU, 2010), 23.

31. Evans, *Power and Ideology*, 1–4.

32. *CIA World Factbook*, https://www.cia.gov/library/publications/the-world-factbook/geos/rs.html. See also Timothy Heleniak, "Russia's Population Perils," in Wegren and Herspring, *After Putin's Russia*, 133–58.

33. Anatoly Vishnevsky and Sergey Bobyley, eds., *National Human Development Report, Russian Federation, 2008: Russia Facing Demographic Challenges* (Moscow: United Nations Development Program, 2009), 24, http://hdr.undp.org/en/reports/nationalreports/europethecis/russia/NHDR_Russia_2008_Eng.pdf. A team of Russia's leading demographers exclusively compiled the report. See also Remington, *Politics in Russia*, 218.

34. Inozemtsev, "Dilemmas of Russia's Modernization," in Krastev, Leonard, and Wilson, *What Does Russia Think?*, 47.

35. Stephen K. Wegren, "Agriculture in the Late Putin Period and Beyond," in Wegren and Herspring, *After Putin's Russia*, 213.

36. Sergei Kulikov, "Dve bol'shiye strategicheskiye raznitsy" [Two huge strategic differences], *Nezavisimaya Gazeta*, March 23, 2011.

37. Anastasiya Bashkatova and Mikhail Sergeev, "Abstraknaya Modernizatsiya ne vyzyvaet doveriya" [Abstract Modernization Evokes No Trust], *Nezavisimaya Gazeta*, March 25, 2011.
38. Aslund, Guriev, and Kuchins, eds., *Russia After the Economic Crisis*, xii.
39. Frances Williams and Charles Clover, "Russia Scraps WTO Customs Bid," *Financial Times*, October 15, 2009, 4.
40. Richard Rousseau, "Russia's WTO Membership on Track or Not?" *Johnson's Russia List* no. 55, March 24, 2011, item 17, http://www.cdi.org/russia/johnson /russia-wto-623.cfm.
41. Economist Intelligence Unit, *Democracy Index 2011*, 23.
42. For a compatible analysis, see Parag Khanna, *The Second World: Empires and Influence in the New Global Order* (New York: Random House, 2008), 10–15, 71–75.
43. "Russia's 2011 GDP Growth to Reach 4.3% in 2011–IMF," *RIA Novosti*, December 9, 2010, http://en.rian.ru/business/20101209/161704360.html.
44. Dmitri Trenin, *Integratsiya i identichnost': Rossiya kak "novyi Zapad"* [Integration and identity: Russia as the "new West"] (Moscow: Evropa, 2006).
45. Sobchak, *Dyuzhina nozhei v spinu*, 129.
46. Russian president Medvedev has employed the term "legal nihilism" in describing Russia's legal tradition. See Medvedev's interview with German journalists, Ivan Dmitriyev, "Doveritel'no: Dmitry Medvedev dal interv'yu nemetski, zhurnalistam" [Confidentially: Dmitry Medvedev Gave an Interview to German Journalists], *Rossiyskaya Gazeta*, August 10, 2007.

SELECTED BIBLIOGRAPHY

Ambrosio, Thomas. "Insulating Russia from a Colour Revolution: How the Kremlin Resists Regional Democratic Trends." *Democratization* 14, no. 2 (April 2007): 232–52.

Aslund, Anders, Sergei Guriev, and Andrew C. Kuchins, eds. *Russia After the Global Economic Crisis.* Washington, DC: Peterson Institute for International Economics, Center for Strategic and International Studies; Moscow: New Economic School, June 2010.

Baev, Pavel K. *Russian Energy Policy and Military Power: Putin's Quest for Greatness.* London: Routledge, 2008.

Balzer, Harley. "The Putin Thesis and Russian Energy Policy." *Post-Soviet Affairs* 21, no. 3 (2005): 210–25.

Blotskiy, Oleg. *Vladimir Putin: Doroga k vlasti* [Vladimir Putin: The road to power]. Moscow: Osmos Press, 2002.

———. *Vladimir Putin: Istoriya zhizni* [Vladimir Putin: The story of his life]. Moscow: Mezhdunarodnye Otnosheniya, 2002.

Bobylev, Sergey N., et al. *National Human Development Report in the Russian Federation, 2009: Energy Sector and Sustainable Development.* Moscow: United Nations Development Program, 2010. http://hdr.undp.org/en/reports/nationalreports /europethecis/russia/NHDR_2009_Russia_English.pdf.

Bressler, Mike L., ed. *Understanding Contemporary Russia.* Boulder, CO: Lynne Rienner, 2009.

Carnaghan, Ellen. *Out of Order: Russian Political Values in an Imperfect World.* University Park: Pennsylvania State University Press, 2007.

Chivers, C. J. "Below Surface, U.S. Has Dim View of Putin and Russia." *New York Times,* December 2, 2010. Contains e-links to select Wikileaks documents summarizing views of U.S. and allied officials on Putin's government, at http:// www.nytimes.com/2010/12/02/world/europe/02wikileaks-russia.html.

European Union. *Report of the Independent International Fact-Finding Mission on the Conflict in Georgia.* September 30, 2009. http://www.cehig/Report.html.

Evans, Alfred B., Jr. *Power and Ideology: Vladimir Putin and the Russian Political System.* Carl Beck Papers, no. 1902. Pittsburgh, PA: University of Pittsburgh, Center for Russian and East European Studies, 2008.

Freedom House. *Freedom in the World, 2010.* Washington, DC: Freedom House, 2011. http://www.freedomhouse.org/template.cfm?page=505.

———. *Nations in Transit, 2010.* Washington, DC: Freedom House, 2010. http://www.freedomhouse.org/template.cfm?page=551.

Guillemoles, Alain, and Alla Lazareva. *Gazprom: Le nouvel empire.* Paris: Les Petits Matins, 2008.

King, William, and David Cleland. *Strategic Planning and Policy.* New York: Van Nostrand Reinhold, 1978.

Klaus, Ulrich G., and Thomas Waelde. "The Role of State Control over Natural Resources and the Economy in Russia: Some Salient Issues in President Putin's Academic Writing." In *The Uppsala Yearbook of East European Law*, edited by Kaj Hobér, 267–92. London: Wildy, Simmonds & Hill Publishing, 2006.

Kolosov, V. A., ed. *Mir glazami Rossiyan: Mify i vneshnyaya politika* [The world through Russians' eyes: Myths and foreign policy]. Moscow: Institut fonda obshchest-vennogo mneniya, 2003.

Kryshtanovskaya, Olga. *Anatomiya rossiyskoy elity* [Anatomy of the Russian elite]. Moscow: Zakharov, 2005.

Lorrain, Pierre. *L'Incroyable alliance Russie–Etas-Unis.* Paris: Editions du Rocher, 2002.

———. *La mystérieuse ascension du Vladimir Poutine.* Paris: Editions du Rocher, 2000, 2002.

Lukic, Reneo, ed. *Conflit et coopération dans les relations Franco-Américaines.* Quebec: Les Presses de l'Université Laval, 2009.

Lynch, Allen C. "The Putin Succession and Russian Foreign Policy." *The Brown Journal of World Affairs* 14, no. 1 (Fall/Winter 2007): 53–64.

March, Luke. "Managing Opposition in a Hybrid Regime: Just Russia and Para-statal Opposition." *Slavic Review* 68, no. 3 (Fall 2009): 504–27.

Mazo, Boris. *Preemnik Putina, ili Kogo my budem vybirat' v 2008 godu* [Putin's succes-sor, or whom are we going to vote for in 2008?]. Moscow: Algoritm, 2005.

Medvedev, Roy. *Vladimir Putin: Chetyre goda v Kremle* [Vladimir Putin: Four years in the Kremlin]. Moscow: Vremya, 2004.

———. *Vladimir Putin: Vtoroy srok* [Vladimir Putin: The second term]. Moscow: Vremya, 2006.

Mendras, Marie, ed. "La Russie de Poutine," special edition of *Pouvoirs. Revue Fran-caise d'Etudes Constitutionnelles et Politiques* no. 112. Paris: Seuil, 2005.

Menon, Rajan, and Alexander J. Motyl. "The Myth of Russian Resurgence." *The American Interest Online*, March–April 2007. http://www.the-american-interest.com/article.cfm?piece=258.

Migranyan, Andranik. "What Is Putinism?" *Russia in Global Affairs* 17, no. 2 (April 13, 2004): 25. http://eng.globalaffairs.ru/number/n–2902.

Mlechin, Leonid. *Kreml': Prezidenty Rossii: Strategiya vlasti ot B. N. El'tsina do V. V. Putina* [The Kremlin: Presidents of Russia: The strategy of power from Yeltsin to Putin]. Moscow: Tsentrpoligraf, 2003.

Mommsen, Margareta, and Angelika Nussberger. *Das System Putin: Gelenkte Demokratie und politische Justiz in Russland.* Munich: C. H. Beck, 2007.

Müller, Konrad Rufus, and Katja Gloger. *Wladimir Putin.* Goettingen, Germany: Steidl Gerhard Verlag, 2003.

Nemtsov, Boris, and Vladimir Milov. *Nezavisimiy ekspertni doklad: Putin: Itogi.* [Putin: The Results: An independent experts report]. Moscow: Novaya Gazeta, 2008.

Piontovsky, Andrei. *Another Look into Putin's Soul.* Translated by Arch Tait. Edited and annotated by David Satter. Washington, DC: Hudson Institute, 2006.

Politkovskaya, Anna. *Putin's Russia.* London: Harvill Press, 2004.

Putin, Vladimir Vladimirovich. *First Person: An Astonishingly Frank Self-Portrait by Russia's President.* Translated by Catherine Fitzpatrick. New York: Public Affairs, 2000.

———. *Izbrannye rechi i vystupleniya* [Selected speeches and addresses]. Moscow: Knizhnyi mir, 2008.

———. "Strategic Planning for Rehabilitation of the Mineral Resources Base of the Region during the Formation of Market Relations." *The Uppsala Yearbook of East European Law.* Edited by Kaj Hobér, 301–478. Translated by Kaj Hobér. London: Wildy, Simmonds & Hill Publishing, 2006.

Rahr, Alexander. *Putin nach Putin: Das kapitalistische Russland am Beginn einer neuen Weltordunung.* Munich: Universitas-Verlag, 2008.

Ravanello, Olivier. *L'oeil de Moscou.* Paris: Les editions du Toucan, 2008.

Reitschuster, Boris. *Putins Demokratur: Wie der Kreml den Westen das Fuerchten lehrt.* Berlin: Ullstein, 2006.

Remington, Thomas F. *Politics in Russia.* 7th ed. Boston: Longman, 2012.

Robertson, Graeme B. "Managed Society: Protest, Civil Society, and Regime in Putin's Russia." *Slavic Review* 68, no. 3 (Fall 2009): 528–47.

Sakwa, Richard. *Putin: Russia's Choice.* London: Routledge, 2004; second edition, 2007.

———. *The Quality of Freedom: Khodorkovsky, Putin, and the Yukos Affair.* Oxford, UK: Oxford University Press, 2009.

Shevtsova, Lilia. *Russia, Lost in Transition: The Yeltsin and Putin Legacies.* Translated by Arch Tait. Washington, DC: Carnegie Endowment for International Peace, 2007.

Sobchak, Anatoly. *Dyuzhina nozhei v spinu* [A dozen knives in the back]. Moscow: Vagrius, 1999.

Solovyov, Vladimir. *Putin: Putevoditel' dlya neravnodushnykh* [Putin: A Guide for those who cannot stay indifferent]. Moscow: Eksmo, 2008.

Solovyov, Vladimir, and Nikolay Zlobin. *Putin-Medvedev: Chto dal'she?* [Putin-Medvedev: What Next?]. Moscow: Eksmo, 2010.

Tinguy, Anne de, Vladimir Baranovsky, Isabelle Facon, and Anaïs Marin, eds. *Moscou et le monde: L'ambition de la grandeur: Une illusion?* Paris: CERI/Autrement, 2008.

Transparency International. *Corruption Perceptions Index 2010.* Berlin: Transparency International, 2010. http://www.transparency.org/policy_research/surveys_indices/cpi/2010.

Trenin, Dmitri. *Integratsiya i identichnost': Rossiya kak "novyi Zapad"* [Integration and identity: Russia as the "new West"]. Moscow: Evropa, 2006.

Truscott, Peter. *Putin's Progress: A Biography of Russia's Enigmatic President, Vladimir Putin.* London: Simon & Schuster, 2004.

Tsygankov, Andrei. "Vladimir Putin's Vision of Russia as a Normal Great Power." *Post-Soviet Affairs* 21, no. 2 (April–June 2005): 132–58.

Vishnevsky, Anatoly, and Sergey Bobylev, eds. *National Human Development Report, Russian Federation, 2008: Russia Facing Demographic Challenges.* Moscow: United Nations Development Program, 2009. http://hdr.undp.org/en/reports/national reports/europethecis/russia/NHDR_Russia_2008_Eng.pdf.

Wegren, Stephen K., and Dale R. Herspring, eds. *After Putin's Russia: Past Imperfect, Future Uncertain.* 4th ed. Lanham, MD: Rowman & Littlefield, 2010.

Wilson, Andrew. *Virtual Politics: Faking Democracy in the Post-Soviet World.* New Haven, CT: Yale University Press, 2005.

Wolton, Thierry. *Le KGB au pouvoir: Le système Poutine.* Paris: Buchet/Chastel, 2008.

The World Bank. *Doing Business.* Washington, DC: The World Bank, 2010. http://www.doingbusiness.org/.

Yeltsin, Boris. *Prezidentskiy marafon* [Presidential marathon]. Moscow: AST, 2000.

Zen'kovich, Nikolai, ed. *Putinskaya entsiklopediya* [The Putin encyclopedia]. Moscow: OLMA Media Grupp, 2008.

INDEX

155

ABOUT THE AUTHOR

Allen C. Lynch is Director of Research, Center for International Studies, and a professor of politics at the University of Virginia. He is the former director of the university's Center for Russian and East European Studies (1993–2008) and former assistant director of the Harriman Institute at Columbia University (1989–1992). He is the author of several books, including *How Russia Is Not Ruled: Reflections on Russian Political Development* (2005) and *Does Russia Have a Democratic Future?* (1997). He lives in Charlottesville, Virginia.